THE
BRIDGE TO
FORGIVENESS

ALSO BY KARYN D. KEDAR

God Whispers
  Stories of the Soul, Lessons of the Heart

Our Dance with God
  Finding Prayer, Perspective and Meaning in the
  Stories of Our Lives
  (In hardcover as *The Dance of the Dolphin*)

THE
BRIDGE TO
FORGIVENESS

stories and prayers for
finding God and
restoring wholeness

KARYN D. KEDAR

For People of All Faiths, All Backgrounds
JEWISH LIGHTS Publishing
Woodstock, Vermont

The Bridge to Forgiveness:
Stories and Prayers for Finding God and Restoring Wholeness

2007 First Printing
© 2007 by Karyn D. Kedar

Grateful acknowledgment is given for permission to reprint "*Esa Enai*—I Lift My Eyes" found in *Nishmat Tzedakah: A Righteous Soul,* Cantor Chayim Frenkel, Executive Producer. Kehillat Israel: Pacific Palisades, CA. 2003:16.

The poem "Learning to Yield" on pp. 111–112 originally appears in *The Women's Seder Sourcebook: Rituals & Readings for Use at the Passover Seder,* ed. by Rabbi Sharon Cohen Anisfeld, Tara Mohr, and Catherine Spector, Jewish Lights Publishing, Woodstock, Vermont, © 2003, ISBN-13: 978-1-58023-232-6, ISBN-10: 1-58023-232-9.

Library of Congress Cataloging-in-Publication Data
Kedar, Karyn D., 1957–
  The bridge to forgiveness : stories and prayers for finding God and restoring wholeness / Karyn D. Kedar.
      p. cm.
  ISBN-13: 978-1-58023-324-8
  ISBN-10: 1-58023-324-4
  1. Forgiveness—Religious aspects—Judaism. 2. Spiritual life—Judaism. 3. Jewish ethics. I. Title.
  BJ1286.F67K43 2007
  296.7'2—dc22

2006036353

10 9 8 7 6 5 4 3 2 1

Manufactured in the United States of America
❀ Printed on recycled paper

Jacket Design: Jenny Buono

For People of All Faiths, All Backgrounds
Published by Jewish Lights Publishing
A Division of Longhill Partners, Inc.
Sunset Farm Offices, Route 4, P.O. Box 237
Woodstock, VT 05091
Tel: (802) 457-4000   Fax: (802) 457-4004
www.jewishlights.com

To my little brother
Neil Dion Schwartz
1958–2002
And to Skyla and Jacob, his grandchildren

Soon after her grandfather died, a little girl said to her grandmother, "Look Bubbe, see that star in the sky? That's Papa smiling at me."

Once, the night sky was opaque with clouds.

"Where's Papa?" the little girl asked.

"Papa is playing a game with us," her grandmother said.

"Tonight he is hiding, tomorrow he will be found."

It's like that sometimes.

CONTENTS

ACKNOWLEDGMENTS

Stuart M. Matlins, publisher. Visionary.

Emily Wichland, vice president of editorial and production. Deliberate, talented.

Jessica Swift, assistant editor. Strong and gentle.

My editor, Arthur Magida. Your editing skills astound.

Congregation B'nai Jehoshua Beth Elohim. My spiritual home. And to the members who kept saying, "Write. Are you writing?" And to the leadership: a sacred partnership. You are compassionate, intelligent, and visionary. Your children and grandchildren will sing your praises. And to Mike and Patti Frazin for a sanctuary in the snow.

My colleagues, who support, create, and conspire to bring sacredness into this world. And to the office staff, who maintain a steady foundation from which to work. And Lori Klark and Sonny Helmer who copy proofed an early manuscript.

Sustainers: Lisa Fisher, David Gottlieb, Kelly Goldberg. Carol Dovi Odwyer. Chuck Rosenberg. Rachel Rosenberg. Arna Yastrow. Steve Yastrow: enduring friendship. Creative synergy. Partners. The competitive edge. Discerning eye, gentle hand. Love.

Ezra. You are my base camp, as I climb the mysterious mountain of the spirit.

ACKNOWLEDGMENTS

Norman and Lynore Schwartz. The beginning of my life and the love that makes it work.

My children, Talia and Moti, Shiri, Ilan. Divine sparks of grace and blessing.

I was reading to Ilan, my fifteen-year-old son, the section of the book about him.

"Is this still about me?" he asked.

"Well, it started out about you and then went to forgiveness."

"Oh," he said. "I sort of dozed off at the end ... It's an adult book, though, right?"

It's like that sometimes.

LIKE A STRAND OF HAIR

I'VE WANTED TO WRITE ABOUT FORGIVENESS for years now. I even pitched it to my publisher a long time ago. "Write it," he said. "I have someone I need to forgive." *Don't we all,* I thought. But it has remained an idea, an item on a very long list. I had sketchy outlines, and vague charts, and a bit of research, and even a diagram of a bridge, a sort of map leading us down the right path where we could confront others and confront ourselves. But it didn't come alive. It had no flesh; it had no soul. Yet occasionally I would hear a voice: Just how do I forgive?

Then one morning, this book took its first breath. It was kind of like an exhalation. Or maybe it was a sigh. Or perhaps it was more like a whisper, a near thought. All morning, I brushed it out of the way. It was elusive, like a feather floating by, rising and dipping as I tried to reach for it. Then it became persistent and annoying, like a lone strand of hair on the back of my tongue, like one of those thoughts that nag until you can no longer ignore it.

Write. About forgiveness. Write. A subtle echo of new life. Write.

Then the phone rang and it was my daughter Talia, calling me on her nineteenth birthday.

Talia, you're nineteen years old. Do you know what that means?

No, Mom. What does it mean?

It means you are almost twenty! Do you know what that means?

No, Mom. What?

It means that soon you get to begin healing.

What!?

Listen, dear. The first twenty years, you grow up. The second twenty years, you heal from growing up. Now listen carefully ...

Yes ...?

By the time you're forty, get over it. We are human, and many mistakes were made in your growing up. Take the next twenty years to heal, and then move on. By then, you are what you are and you aren't what you are not.

Mommm!!

OK, dear. Happy birthday!

Thanks, Mom.

This book is what occurs to me at the end of my second twenty years ...

THE BRIDGE

Forgiveness is a path to be walked.
There are steps along the way:
loss, anger, acceptance, learning,
forgiveness, restoration.

And along the way, you will come upon a bridge.
When you step upon it, it will carry you,
support you, connect you to another side of life,
a side waiting to be discovered.

Forgiveness is a perpetual journey.
There are many bridge crossings.
Each restores a bit more of what you have lost.

Begin.

THE STEPPING-STONES

FORGIVENESS IS A LIKE A BRIDGE. It carries you over an expanse to the side of life that is softer, kinder, easier to bear. It is a shift of perspective, a new way of seeing our world, a different way of experiencing our inner life. If life is really a journey, then forgiveness is a main avenue, a path to life renewed. And along the way, there are stepping-stones to carry you through: loss, anger, acceptance, forgiveness, learning, and restoration. With each step, a new perspective is gained.

Forgiveness is often understood as an act of unselfish, unconditional love, an act in which we learn to "forgive and forget," maybe even to "turn the other cheek." That is not what is described in this book. After bearing witness to evil such as the Holocaust, genocide, and other acts of terror, we search for a new paradigm. There should be no forgetting of evil acts, no condoning of offense, sin, hatred. To forget is to run the risk of allowing these evils to happen again. Yet at the same time, to hold within us the horror and pain of every offense diminishes our lives. Resentment, anger, and fear must be released from within us so that we may restore our inner light, regain a sense of life's purpose, and reinvigorate our energy and optimism, so we can live with goodness and love.

I have come to understand that this journey, this path, this way of being in the world has many stages. They are stepping-stones in a journey that is perpetual and unending. Each step restores a bit more of what we have lost. Each step leads to greater wisdom and understanding, to a deeper sense of life's meaning and purpose. We do not forget. Rather, we take what we have experienced and learn to live a different way. We do not turn the other cheek; we take the pain of an assault and understand that to live a loving life we must release the anger. We do not condone; we accept our lives and search for ways to restore the light within us that has been diminished.

Every offense leads to a sense of *loss*. A bit of wholeness is cracked or chipped or shattered. We lose a bit of trust, security, or faith. Or some of our sense of wonder. Every pain inflicted upon us may cause us to lose our way, to forget the meaning and purpose of our lives. But mostly with every hurt, the light that is within us is darkened or dimmed.

Understandably, loss creates *anger*. We are justified in our anger when we experience hurt and pain. We are certainly jus-tified in being angry at the injustices of the world. I have come to believe that anger is a necessary step toward forgiveness; without it, there is a certain denial or repression. But anger is also dangerous. Though we must feel the anger, we must also know when to release it before it consumes us. We must learn to turn anger into motivation, lest it devour us. We long to rid the world of insanity, to rid our lives of all that is not good, of whatever does not serve the good in us. The search for God is the fight to relieve ourselves and the world of suffering. With every breath, we inhale the possibility of healing and of holi-ness. Loss then becomes anger, and anger can then motivate us toward change. And once we can release the anger that we have felt, we can begin to understand the need for acceptance.

To live life fully is to accept what has become of you. *Acceptance* is not acquiescence. It is not giving in, and it is not giving up. Acceptance is the compassionate embrace of yourself and your place in the world: without judgment, without fear, without regret. You are who you are. You are not who you are not. Every story has pain and loss and, despite all this, our life force is resilient. The soul yearns to reconcile the curses and the blessings of life by finding meaning and purpose. Everything that you have experienced has led you to this moment in time. And this moment in time has the potential to be filled with blessing and with an awareness of life's wonders and miracles.

Forgiveness is not condoning the wrong in the world or the offenses we experience in our lives. It is not forgetting. Forgiveness is a state of being. It is a bridge that carries us over the hurt we have experienced, leading us to a life of greater peace and acceptance. If you step upon it, it will carry you, support you, and connect you to another side of life, a side waiting to be discovered.

Always, there is the bridge to be crossed—an arch high above an abyss of fear and mistrust that carries you away from loss and anger and toward more acceptance, toward a life of learning. We can *learn* from everything that life presents to us. We learn from loss, from anger, from survival, from perseverance. Life is learning and growing.

And in the learning is an opportunity for *restoration*. You can restore your faith, your trust, your optimism, your sense of beauty. You do not go back to the way you were when life seemed simpler, because now you know that life is not simple. It is a complicated path of pain and joy, of disappointment and achievement, of betrayal and love. And now that you know that, and accept the impact that it has on you, you can regain a sense of wholeness and restore the light within.

It's a Matter of Principle

THE "BRIDGE TO FORGIVENESS" IS A METAPHOR for a spiritual principle. Spiritual principles are not visible to the eye. They are only visible to the heart and soul. They are love ... hope ... patience ... forgiveness. These are the forces that make life work. Unlike physical laws, spiritual principles sometimes elude the rational mind because often they do not add up. How can you love in the face of despair, or forgive the undeserving, or give abundantly when there doesn't seem to be enough forgiveness to go around? These principles are not mathematical equations, neatly calculated like algebra. And yet, they are as real as gravity or centrifugal force. When you yield to their power, you feel as if you are standing firmly upon the ground—centered, balanced, and upright.

Spiritual principles allow us to touch the great mystery of existence.

They are the answer to the eternal questions.

They are the laws that govern the invisible ... the ineffable ... and the intangible.

They are life's light, eternally true, and eternally holy.

They are the will of the Divine.

They banish darkness, fear, deception, and profound sadness.

They are like stepping-stones that cross over a rapid river.

Step carefully and you can safely cross without being swept away.

They are revealed, and are simple and complex at the same time.

They are as plain as the nose on your face.

And, like your face, they are seen upon reflection.

They are as beautiful as a spider's web, waiting to capture your heart.

They are love, kindness, struggle, abundance.

They allow us to do justly, to love mercy, and to walk humbly with God.

Forgiveness is a spiritual principle.

It is a bridge that will lead you to the next stage of your life.

MY ROCK

God,
like stones in the river,
carry me across.
You are my Rock
and my Redeemer.

CHOOSING

There is a moment in time where
you see a flash of light, or feel a slight wisp of wind
or notice a momentary pause
as if the world is holding its breath.

And then suddenly, at that moment,
your life comes into focus.
And it is that very moment in time
that beckons you to take a turn in the road
and step on a path that leads you
to the truth of who you are.

And in the moment, in the light,
in the whisper of wind, in the pause,
you have a choice that can change your life forever.
You can choose to live.
To really live
or to simply get along.

Choose to live.

AN INVITATION TO
AN AWAKENING

THE LIGHT BROKE THROUGH THE THICK TANGLE of green overgrowth. It came through the still leaves of the trees. Each time a ray came out from the shadows of predawn—radiance! Sparks of soft light dancing like a prayer, a quiet supplication to stir the life that was slumbering. Wake up. It really is spectacular as the dawn breaks through the night and the sun burns off the mist. Every morning. Every morning.

Every morning, we are invited to witness the emerging day as if it is the beginning of time. The miracle of God's creation, of human endeavor, of a world in perpetual motion, of endless possibility for life renewed. Every morning, a new day. Forgiveness is an early morning walk—it is life long. We step softly through experience, pain, and wonder as if we have found ourselves after being a bit lost in the thick woods. Listen to the calls of the morning; they urge the light to break through. Listen.

Every day that we are alive, there is an invitation to the morning ritual of awakening.

We awake to creation. We awake to our essential self. We awake to a core in our soul so soft and so real that it stirs within us a yearning to become reacquainted with the purpose of our life. And here is what was made known to me this morning: that whatever our purpose, it cannot possibly be for strife and anguish. Whatever our purpose, it must be like the sparks of light at dawn—bright, inviting, unbelievably lovely. The dawn's light calls us to a new day, and on each new day comes a possibility of returning to the truth of who we are. Forgiveness is an important step in that return.

Forgiveness is like the miracle of daybreak, like radiance falling upon the shadows.

LOVE AND FEAR

God sustains the world as a vessel of abundant love.
—GEVUROT PRAYER

THE DAY WAS BAD. I thought of quitting, of running away, of retreating to a safer place. Like a turtle in her shell, scanning the outside world, I wanted to pull back to protect myself against the assault of those around me. So I went to the Botanical Gardens, a sanctuary of nature that always calms the spirit. The tulips were in bloom—evidence of the tenacity of spring despite the nighttime frost that had somehow continued into the month of May. Tenacity. Like the spirit that will not die. Like the life that refuses to give in. Like the world that will not crumble. There were colors of red, gold, white, pale orange, each igniting love in my heart. As I walked among the tulips, escape was no longer an option. Love, not fear, they seemed to say. Love, not fear.

It's like that sometimes.

Life is like a clay vessel filled with a kind of holy love, abundant with divine grace, overflowing with goodness and beauty. Life is not a simple choice between love and hate, with everything sketched out in black and white. Rather, imagine that your life is a choice between love and fear. Fear of what? Fear of not having love—abundant, unconditional love. You see, the spiritual opposite of love is not hate. The opposite of love is fear. Fear that there is a limit to love, to goodness. Fear of confronting a mystery that is essentially unknowable. Fear of letting go, of losing control, of letting others get too close, of living with a sense of godliness. When all those fears dissipate, love fills the void. God, Spirit, Faith, Divine, Holy, and Love are all synonymous with each other, and all are infinite.

And so the question is not, "Is there enough love for you?" Rather, the question is, "Will you choose love over fear?"

Near the Dead Sea is an oasis called Ein Gedi. The summer heat is intense, dry, oppressive. The Dead Sea is utterly still, blue, buoyant, filled with minerals that let nothing live in its waters. And suddenly, off the road in the distance is green and date palms and flowers and shade. Here, there is life. You drive into the parking lot, leave your car, fill your water bottle, and begin climbing a mountain along a path. You pass stones and boulders. There is green, but there is also a stifling heat. Suddenly, you hear people playing, laughing, yelling to one another. You hear water falling on rocks and people splashing. You round the bend, and there it is. A waterfall! You enter the pool and stand in the cool water. All the dust, all the heat, all the deadness washes from your body and you feel alive and filled to the brim with ... love.

The world is like a clay vessel, filled with love's potential. Our choices are to change, to love, to fear. To take a path, or to take a turn. To search for places where there is abundant love that is sustained by a source, deep and invisible, like an oasis in the desert.

Forgiveness is the choice of love over fear.

THE CALL

Out of the night came a noise—soft, faint, distinct enough to wake me from my sleep. There were two brief sounds: *who, who.* They did not arrive in the form of a question, but as a bold statement of truth: *who, who.* I looked at the clock—4:00 a.m. Too late to go back to sleep; too early to wake up. So I lay there and listened for the next call. For a long time, there was silence, as if the night had played a trick on me or maybe a dream had awakened me instead. Then I heard it again, two brief calls in the distance. This time, no emphatic statements of *who,* but rather a soft wooing sound, almost a faraway whisper, a kind of "come hither" that was drawing me into the night. I became scared and poked my sleeping husband.

"Ezra, did you hear that?"

"No."

"Listen."

Silence, silence, silence. Pause. Then *woo, woo.*

"That! Did you hear that?"

"Hmm."

"Are there owls in Illinois?" I asked, wanting to give a name to the nighttime sounds.

"Uh ... yuh," he said, then turned over to go back to sleep, leaving me alone with the night.

It went on like that for quite a while. I lay in my bed, very still, very alert, waiting for a call from someplace out there, wondering what it all meant. The owl would sound, then another type of bird—majestic and melodic. Then silence. Then a plane, a freight train. Then silence, followed by a third bird—this time a rather annoying chirp, many short sounds in rapid succession. I listened to the night chatter, talking to me in a type of code that I could not decipher. During the silences, I looked for meaning. Then the sounds would call out, enchanting me so that I felt drawn into the shadows. And then, just as I thought I might understand what it was all about, moments before the morning light began to crawl into my room, I drifted off to sleep. The night dissipated with the morning dew. The sounds silenced. The calls became a vague memory. I nearly forgot the whole thing. Revelation had called from the darkness, elusive and mysterious. But I, now unaware, was asleep.

Forgiveness can be just that—elusive. From the dark side of your life, you may be called to pay attention, to awaken to goodness and inner peace. But you may not choose to listen. Or you may be unable to decipher the call. Or you may be confused by its mysterious code. So you roll over and fall asleep, not capable of being present in the midst of great meaning and truth.

Forgiveness is like the mysterious call of the night—a call to awaken that which sleeps deep within your soul.

LOSS

We begin with loss.

With every offense, there is a loss ...
Loss of trust, of confidence, of security.
With every injury there is more loss ...
of self, of faith, of hope.
There is a loss of inner light.

Acknowledge what is gone so that you can begin
to find it again.

FORGIVENESS IS NOT
AN EMOTION

Forgiveness leads to the restoration of what we have lost.

It is unfortunate that, when speaking of forgiveness, so much of the focus is on the person who has offended you. It's as if to forgive is to redeem the soul of another, to somehow accept his or her behavior, to move on and forget. What if the offender does not change? What if the offender has passed away and reconciliation is not possible? What if the other is no longer a part of your life, yet what remains from your encounter with that person still lingers in your soul? If our focus is on the offender, then our chance to redeem what we have lost may slip away from us.

We simply have too much to lose. The stakes are high. With every insult and with every assault, we lose trust and faith and our belief that life could be different. We lose our innocence, the belief that life is essentially good and fair. So much of forgiveness is about finding what was lost, about restoring the wholeness that we once had. It is a coming to terms with the story of our life. Forgiveness does not spontaneously bubble forth, erasing all evil and wounds. It involves intention, purpose, vision. It is a path to be discovered, an expectation that there is another side to the pain and diminishment that we have suffered.

Forgiveness is a spiritual state, a way of being in the world that is sustainable with work and practice. Forgiveness can be about the other, but not necessarily. It can be about reconciling with whoever has offended you. But not necessarily. It is always about finding what you have lost, restoring a sense of wholeness, redeeming your inner light. It is always about an internal process of loss and acceptance, pain and understanding, anger and blessings, love and faith regained.

PATH IN THE ICE

I took a walk to find some air and found, instead,
a chill that lives in the marrow.
The sky was colorless,
lifeless; no bird, no insect, no visible sun or moving cloud.
Even the Monarch slept.
The earth, the land, the hills, the path
all void of bloom, muddy and soggy from winter.

The lake was frozen
though the mallards seemed to find a path.
"Keep moving," I whispered to them.
"Just keep moving.
All this is fleeting. Keep moving.
Despite it all, find the stream that flows."

Then, suddenly, as if they heard my supplication,
they turned toward me. One after another in a line
following the leader, they came ashore.
I sat awhile and watched them do what ducks tend to do.

The wind picked up, the chill thickened, and I thought,
I must forgive what was. I simply have too much to lose:
dignity, trust, my dreams, a sense of self,
faith, love, imagination,
joy, confidence,
God.

Then just as quickly as they came ashore,
They returned to the pond.
"Keep moving," I whispered to them.
"Just keep moving.
All this is fleeting. Keep moving.
Despite it all, find the stream that flows."

Forgiveness is like a stream in a winter pond. It finds a path through the ice. Keep moving forward toward goodness and love. Keep moving away from hurt, keep moving toward wholeness, so you can regain what you have lost. Let the pain be as fleeting as the winter chill. Let love and wholeness abide. Find the path through the ice.

THE GHOST OF LOVE

THIS MORNING I SAT ALONE, perfectly still in the darkness of an empty sanctuary void of worshipers, of prayer, of music. I listened to the silence, trying to hear the prayers of the many souls that had been there. I wondered, what do they pray when no one is listening? Then, I heard a faint echo. It was like the sound of lives lived in wonder: a choir of sighs and song, of high and low notes, of harmony and dissonance. And in the darkness of the empty sanctuary, I was comforted. I realized that life is not about one painful moment in time. Rather, it is an arc of time. And in that arc, countless souls have prayed and found some small measure of wonder. And despite all the pain, in that small measure of wonder, a light bursts forth.

And in the light—forgiveness.

MOMENTS ARE FINITE,
YET FOREVER

Sᴘʀᴀᴡʟᴇᴅ ᴏᴜᴛ ᴏɴ ᴛʜᴇ ᴄᴏᴜᴄʜ, my son was watching multiple sporting events on television. Frustrated with one game, he would flip to another, or a commercial would come on and he'd flip again. He changed channels with such speed that my middle-aged brain couldn't even register what was passing by. I looked at his lean, long, fourteen-year-old body—the body of my youngest child, now a freshman in high school—and I wondered how he had arrived at this point. He was transformed; his voice, skin, muscles, smell were all different, but his sweetness remained. I detected a rare opportunity to sit with him, maybe hear a bit of what was going on in his life.

"Can I sit down, Ilan?"

"Sure," he said. "Scratch my back?"

"Sure," I answered, "but can we watch something we'd both like?"

"Sure." It was our usual negotiation.

He flipped through sitcoms and hospital shows, finally settling on a detective series. I actually thought that I was paying attention, but then Ilan would say, "Oh my God, can you believe that?" I'd look up and not know what was going on. Or he'd say, "Is that the same guy as before?" And I would have no clue about who any of the guys were. I only knew that my son still allowed me to be close. From his first days of life in the neonatal unit of Hadassah Hospital, where he was in an incubator and attached to breathing machines, IVs, and system monitors, I have lightly, gently, scratched his back. It is as if every time I scratch his back, we both have a memory of the soul, when life and death were blurred and love and hope prevailed.

So here I was, sharply aware of the finite nature of life. Nothing lasts forever. It is all ever changing, ever moving. And in every change, we experience both a loss and a gain. That is the nature of life. As one thing falls away, space is created for another thing to take its place.

I looked down at Ilan. How did I get here? I simply had to keep living. So much of living is unconscious, a thoughtless movement through time. When we live consciously—that is, when we live with intention—then there is a dual sense of reality, a sense of the finite and a sense of the everlasting. On one hand, all moments pass, all things are finite. And just as moments pass in time, so too do they linger on in our spirits and in our memories.

The sting from a bad fall lives on as fear.
Betrayal lives on as distrust.
Consistent criticism lives on as self-doubt.
Love lives on as yearning.
The beauty of a winter day lives on as awe.
Success lives on as confidence.

Forgiveness weaves through our memories to the eternal moments of the soul, easing that which is harsh, resting on that which is gentle.

DIMINISHED LIGHT

In the beginning there was heaven and earth—
And the earth was unformed and void,
With darkness over the surface of the deep
And a wind, the spirit of God
Sweeping over the water—
And God said, "Let there be light"
And there was light.
—GENESIS 1:1

What was this light that was created?
The sun, moon and stars were created only on the fourth day. The
light is the righteousness in those who are yet to come into the world.
—ADAPTED FROM RASHI

Energy is neither created nor destroyed.
—ADAPTED FROM JULIUS ROBERT VON MAYER

THE BEGINNING IS A STORY OF CREATION, of birth. There was darkness, water, unformed void. There was the spirit of God. The universe before creation is like the womb before birth. And then God said, "Let there be light," and the world was birthed into being. This light, we are taught by poets, rabbis, and physicists alike, is still around. It exists as energy, as a particle, as a wave, as goodness within the core of humans. It is waiting to be discovered through some mathematical formula, or viewed through the lens of a telescope, or by metaphor, or through human experience and encounter.

I am perpetually in search of the light.

Just imagine. Imagine you were created in a mysterious and sacred partnership of parents and a divine source. One gave you your body, and the other, your spirit. Imagine that the reason for your creation was to live a life whose purpose was to be and to act in a divine image, to be a partner in creation. To create a sense of divinity on earth, to heal yourself and those you love, to fix a broken world. To live fully with an internal light as a beacon for love and hope and faith and betterment.

Imagine that your soul is your inheritance from the days of creation and that your soul is a brilliant beam of light, beginning from above, running through your mind, into your core, and out through your heart. The light from creation that was never destroyed runs through you. It is eternal, divine, and powerful. It is what was, before you were born, and it is what will be, after you die. And as long as you have breath, it is what gives your life the capacity for holiness and goodness. It contains the great mysteries that you yearn to discover. It holds the secret of godliness and the very reason you were born.

Imagine that.

And so, how would our lives be different if we only believed what we recite in the morning prayers, *"The soul You have given us is a pure one"*? And life becomes a complicated journey. You live among imperfect beings, whose brokenness bumps into you at every turn. And from your earliest days, you begin to hurt; you fall when you try to walk, you are pushed when you begin to reach, you are ignored when you cry. From the beginning, living is a struggle between the beauty and the beast. I don't know why.

It's like that sometimes.

If your soul can be imagined as a brilliant beam of light, originating from above, running through your mind, into your core, and out through your heart, then every offense, every bit of criticism, every attack throughout your life has the capacity to diminish that light, and the dimming of the light within your being is the ultimate loss. It is as if each offense has the potential to form bits of dark crust around that brilliant beam, diminishing the light within. And periodically, the offense is so great that it shatters a bit of your light, splinters the beam like a bone that cannot bear the weight of it all.

Can you imagine your light? Is it darkened or splintered? You have seen light and darkness in others, as they "light up your life" or "light up the room" when they enter. And you have seen the dark in others. It is almost as if they live in a dark cloud.

Every act toward restoring your inner light is a step toward redemption. It is the journey of the spirit. It is the reason and the purpose of your life. To be created in the image of God is to be a creator of worlds, of the small corner of the universe you inhabit. It means that you heal, love, invent, bring joy, create, teach, and love again. It means that you are authentic and strong and powerful. For the truth of who you are is beauty.

In the beginning, there was darkness and unformed void and the spirit of God, and then God said, "Let there be light." And there was. And the poets and the teachers and the physicists and all the rest of us look for that light to this very day.

I say, it is within you, waiting to be redeemed.

Forgiveness is light restored.

The Darkness of the Soul

The darkness of the soul
is like a night in a room
with the blinds drawn and opaque.
Points of light seem
distant and indiscernible from my bed.
The blanket that should warm me is heavy,
suffocating.
Will morning ever come?

Teach me, O God,
to see it differently. Lay me down gently
that I may come to know You.
Let the blanket no longer be suffocating.
Rather, let it be a canopy of peace gently caressing me
and protecting me in the shadow of Your wings.

As I learn forgiveness,
though the blinds stay drawn,
I gently lay down my head and close my eyes
To see the light within my soul restored.

ANGER

There is good reason to be angry.
There is good reason not to be angry.

Anger can be like a river
that swells beyond its banks,
flooding and destroying everything in its path.
Or it can be like a river
that flows through your soul,
washing away all that needs to be gone.

Discernment is
knowing when to be angry and when to let it go.

FORGIVENESS AND EVIL:
A PARADIGM SHIFT

I have set before you this day the blessing and the curse, life and death. Choose life that you may live.
—DEUTERONOMY 30:19

THERE ARE UNFORGIVABLE ACTS. Genocide. Terrorism. Rape. Murder. Abuse. Holocaust. With such horror, there is no series of events separated by a comma. Each is its own reality, too horrible to compare to anything else. Each crime bears witness to the human choice between good and evil. There are people who choose evil. They choose to live and act in darkness and pain and inflict upon others their desire for destruction. In the face of evil, you have the opportunity to choose good. Not to condone evil. Not to turn the other cheek. And never to forget. But rather, to let go of the darkness that has entered your soul. To let go of the control that evil can have over you. To let go of the pain. To let go of the fear. In the face of evil, forgiveness is what you give yourself. It is an essential and primal release of the poison and brokenness that has entered your soul. You acknowledge the loss of innocence, trust, faith, inner light. You rage against the crime that was committed. And you accept, with self-love, the story that has become your life. For you have survived, and your life's path can send you forth to bear witness to the ultimate tenacity and triumph of the good that is in the human spirit. Place the evil in the past; it does not have to be your present reality. Become strong. Then you will let go of the curse over your life, little by little.

While you do not, cannot, forgive evil, you must shift your focus from the offender, and the offense he or she committed, to the deep and undying desire to regain equilibrium and control over your life. Forgiveness is not what you grant another person. Rather, it is a state of mind. Forgiveness is actually a decision about how to live. Forgiveness is regaining control over your life.

Evil and unforgivable acts cause great pain and suffering. They cause a darkness to fall upon your soul. When you choose a forgiving state of being, you enter a state of inner peace by letting go of pain and fear. You choose to leave the darkness that has been your reality, and you regain control over your spirit. Darkness is the arena of evil; it can control your life. Its grip can be as destructive as a hurricane: unrelenting, tenacious.

Forgiveness, on the other hand, is a state where light becomes your reality. You regain control over your spirit, over your memories, over your way of perceiving the world and your way of walking on this planet. Do not be afraid to forgive. Surrender this hell to your past, and embrace the calm as your present reality.

Forgive not the oppressor. But forgive nevertheless. To release the grip of your enemy is an act of redemption. As you redeem your spirit from your oppressor, you restore light from darkness.

To forgive is not to condone or forget. It is the message that goodness can triumph over evil.

THE COMMANDMENT TO ACT

WHEN WE BEAR WITNESS TO EVIL, we know, really know, of its existence and power, and we can never again look at life the same way. To know evil is to be commanded to eradicate it, to act passionately against it, to prevent it from terrorizing anyone, anywhere. When you stand idly by the blood of your neighbor, something inside you dies.

When you know how bad life can be, and you do nothing, it is as if your soul begins to atrophy. The light is dimmed, and that divine spark that is meant for healing flickers and flutters. You cannot do nothing. Doing nothing in the face of evil betrays the life force. It betrays the reason you were born, and it even betrays the pain you have suffered. For with your help, goodness can prevail over evil.

Heal your wounds for the sake of your spirit, for the sake of others who await your healing heart. Let evil stir you to the core and awaken within you compassion for those who suffer. You can speak the language, you can see the monsters, you can know the truth and depth of the pain of others.

You must not be still. Let compassion send you out to redeem a broken world, or at least one broken heart.

MEMORY

Never to forget. Never again.
And yet,
do not allow your memories to become
an angry monster in your soul,
living in the darkness, living, breathing
more real than the real,
so frightening that it lurks beyond the nighttime closet
into the daytime, stalking, crippling,
eclipsing any good, or joy, or light that you could live.

Rather,
may the memory of darkness
help you choose light—
and the memory of curse
help you choose blessing—
and the memory of death
help you choose life …
That you may live,
you and your offspring.

The Paradox of Fire

Definition

Fire: flashing light; luminous appearance. Burning passion;
excitement or enthusiasm. Liveliness of imagination. Severe trial or
trouble; ordeal. A spark. The discharge of firearms; enemy fire.
—The Random House Unabridged Dictionary

Fire is a paradox. It warms. It destroys. It lights our way. It is untamable. It must be respected, watched, tended to. It is a soft flame in a candle lighting a dark room, or a wild, unruly force that turns life into ash. We've known this all our lives, from the day our parents told us not to play with matches.

Anger is like fire. Both are paradoxes that we must learn to manage. You can choose between enthusiasm and criticism. You choose brilliance and luminosity. Or you can attack. You choose light that shines like the facets of a gemstone or settle for a severe test, a trial, or trouble.

Alien Fire

Now Aaron's sons,
Nadab and Abihu,
each took his fire pan and offered before God

an alien fire.
And the fire came forth and consumed them.
And then Mishael and Elzaphan, sons of Uzziel,
The uncle of Aaron
Came forward
And carried them out by their tunics.
—LEVITICUS 10:1–2, 4–5

It's like that sometimes.

What we think will warm us and nourish us, in fact, consumes us like an alien fire. "Alien" because its light is like a torch in the darkness that leads you astray. It convinces you that sadness or anger is worth holding on to. "Alien" because it burns within you like unleashed passion, destroying what is good. "Alien" because it lures you to be estranged and separate, hurt and uninvolved, because it leads you from the true purpose of your life. "Alien" because it consumes all that is good and turns it into black ash.

Nadab and Abihu were pulled from the fire by their tunics. Their tunics did not burn. They died not a physical death, but a spiritual death. This is like anger unleashed.

When anger defines your life, it becomes the essential part of your story. When anger is used to hate and destroy, when it is what you feel in the morning and in the night, when your relationships are rooted in conflict, then anger is like an alien fire that turns your spirit to ash.

We must distinguish between fire that warms us and fire that consumes us. Anger is an important step toward forgiveness. But not all anger, and not all the time.

The Fire of Mystery

> *And Moses was tending the flock*
> *Of his father-in-law Jethro and drove the flock*
> *Into the wilderness.*
> *An Angel of God appeared to him*
> *In a blazing fire*
> *Out of a bush.*
> *He gazed,*
> *And there was a bush all aflame,*
> *Yet the bush was not consumed.*
> *And God called out to him and said,*
> *"Remove your sandals, for the place on which you stand*
> *is holy ground."*
> —EXODUS 3:1–5

The fire of revelation burns all around us. It is light. It is nourishment. It guides us through the darkness, allowing us to feel deeply and passionately all that there is to be felt. It does not consume. Instead, it calls us to realize a life that is purposeful.

For much of our lives, we are lost in our pain or lost in our anger. It is as if we live in an undiscovered wilderness. We are unaware. Our inner life is a place that is vast, uncultivated, frightening, and yet beautiful. Although it lives within us, it is a foreign land. We do not explore it; we do not try to understand it. We do not even really know it. It just is a fact. It is the landscape of our soul.

But there are miracles all around. Our inner world is like fire, with all its complexities and all its paradoxes.

Then, periodically, we are called to the wilderness. This is rarely gentle. Calls into the wilderness are usually dramatic. They pull us forth from complacency. And sometimes, something happens that shakes us up so completely, that it feels like tragedy. Normal life disappears and we struggle to find our balance, to regain our composure.

We hold on to what we know, even when what we know is hard or painful. This is an oddity of human nature, and that is why it seems easier *not* to forgive. Non-forgiveness is what we know. Forgiveness seems like a step into uncharted territory, into the wilderness.

Nevertheless, periodically, we are called.

We can be called like Aaron's sons to an alien fire. Or we can be called, like Moses, to step into the wilderness of our fears, into our estrangement from life's purpose, and to see that life is awesome—filled with wonder that is safe, nourishing, and commanding. Then we know that the ordinary ground beneath our feet is sacred.

Forgiveness is the call to beware of the fire that destroys and to warm yourself by the fire that ignites holiness in your heart and that rekindles life's purpose.

LIGHT AND WARMTH

God,
may the passion of all that is good in life burn within my heart.
My heart yearns for light and warmth.
May I be guided to feel fully and deeply,
fighting the injustice in the world while
loving peace and harmony.

By Your light, O God,
may I see light.

THE CASE FOR ANGER

SHE SAT DOWN AND IMMEDIATELY BEGAN TO CRY. I looked at her as she dove right into her tale. No introduction, no formalities. Straight into the pain and horror of her story: Abuse. It was truly horrible. It was our third or fourth meeting. I found myself staring at her sadness, trying to imagine her another way: laughing, or shopping, or playing with her children, or bored, or making dinner. It was hard.

"Where's God?" she asked. "Where was God?"

"Have you gotten angry?" I answered. "Have you tried getting angry at God?"

"Get angry at God?" she repeated as if the thought had never really occurred to her.

"It's OK to get angry," I said. "Angry at your father, your mother. Angry at God. If you are looking for faith, it might be on the other side of your anger. But to get to the other side, you need to pass through anger."

She was quiet. I tried to imagine her putting on lipstick to go to dinner and a movie. I tried to imagine her walking through the ordinary moments of life in an ordinary way. I held her in my heart as a vision of wholeness.

Your anger belongs to you. You can do with it as you wish. If it is neglected or avoided, it can lay heavy on your soul. But if you allow it to surface, and face it without fear and walk into the center of it, it can heal. Well-placed anger is a healing agent. It tells you that what happened is wrong. Really wrong. It reminds you that you did not deserve the offense. Anger can restore a sense of self, a sense of self-worth. It allows the victim in you to disappear. It is a good and necessary part of the walk toward forgiveness.

What is unfair is unfair. What is unjust is unjust. Say this plainly. Feel it profoundly.

A victim is a person who feels less than whole. Anger can transform a victim into a person who believes he or she deserves goodness, wholeness, and love. Forgiveness cannot come without feeling anger.

Feel the anger.

But not forever.

LIFE DEFINED

If you stay angry forever
the one who has wronged you will win.
If you hold on to your anger
as self-defense or
as self-protection,
eventually you will lose
because the pain of that anger will begin
to define you.

Love life.
And allow the loving presence
of the Spirit of the Universe to
live in your core.
Love life.
And its wonders and miracles
will give you renewed purpose for living.

SEARCHING FOR FOCUS

After Rabbi Moshe from Kovrin died,
one of his disciples happened to be with
Rabbi Mendel from Kotzek.
The tzaddik *asked him,*
"What was the essential teaching of your rabbi?"
The student contemplated the question
for a short time and answered,
"Whatever he was considering at the moment."
—MARTIN BUBER, OR HAGANUZ

YOU CANNOT LINGER LONG IN THE WORLD OF ANGER. It is too powerful, and its power can destroy all that is good. You must shift your focus. Here is the spiritual principle: You get what you focus on. If your heart is consumed with anger, then your life will be consumed with anger, too.

Focus. This morning, the sunlight turned the treetops golden. I stared at their loveliness for quite a while, until I saw the entire world as if it were kissed by gold. As I meditated on the light, I considered all that is golden in my life; recounting my blessings, I focused on the tips of the trees, and I saw them transform into a treasure chest of gold—each piece counted as the richness that has become my life.

Focus. Like trying to avoid the silly behavior of the person next to you. "Ignore it," you say to yourself. "Just ignore it." By getting swept away by it, you are actually focusing on exactly what you claim you want to avoid: The blemish on the other person's nose, the low-cut neckline on her dress, the annoying behavior of your toddler, the open zipper of the man talking to you, or the itch that you simply should not scratch. Your focus is so intense that it leads you to distraction.

Focus. Driving my car on a suburban street, I was deep in thought, barely paying attention to the road ahead. The car just seemed to be driving itself. Then suddenly, out of the corner of my eye, I noticed children playing along the side of the road. One boy, in particular, caught my attention. He was so exuberant playing with his ball, so cute, so oblivious to my oncoming car. I focused on his every move, every catch, every jump. *Pay attention,* I silently said to him. *Don't run into the street. Be careful. Don't run into the street.* Then unexpectedly, there was a curve in the road, and my car, instead of turning, continued toward the object of my attention. I quickly swerved away from the boy, who never left the grassy strip, and I refocused my attention on the road ahead.

Focus:

If your mind is distracted by the past,
it becomes your present.

Concentrate:

Meditate on creating something new in your life.
Focus on letting go, on looking beyond the anger,
on forgiveness,

on bringing blessing into your life,
and you won't be able to avoid those things any longer.

Focus is what we do with our attention. Attention is a powerful spiritual principle.

Forgiveness demands a shift of attention.

AMEN: SAYING "YES"

CAN WE CONTROL THE EVENTS that take place in our lives? Sometimes, yes. Sometimes, no. Can we control our reaction to them? Always. It's hard, but it is within our control to react, to believe, to respond, to feel, to behave, to form an opinion about what happens to us, to build scenarios. It is within our power to create within our souls a picture of what life means. So powerful is the mind and the spirit that it is as if we are having a constant conversation with life, a conversation that affirms what we tell it. Say "yes" when your heart and soul affirm the loving truth of life. It is the answer to hope and to your unlimited capacity for love.

"Yes" is open, wide open, like a crack in the earth that reveals the depths of existence.

"Yes" does not mean that there is no pain. It means that there is more to pain than the pain itself, that there are blessings within the pain, and wisdom beyond the pain, and life beyond the pain. "And God said yes" is not a metaphor for the granting of three wishes, like the "abracadabra" of our childhood fantasies. "Yes" affirms that life can be good despite our struggles, that peace can be made despite our conflicts, that healing can overcome our pain. When we accept the divine purpose in our lives, it is as if all that is holy and good says "amen."

What we believe to be true, we prove to be true, whether it is or not. There is such enormous power in our attitudes and in our minds that we tend to affirm and manifest our beliefs. We think that we are objectively looking at things, but what we are actually doing is gathering evidence to prove that what we believe to be true is true. We state our intention and the answer returns to us as *yes*.

The universe conspires with you to fulfill your destiny.

So the conversation with the world goes something like this:

They are out to get me. *Yes.*

I will be betrayed. *Yes.*

He's just going to fight with me. *Yes.*

I'll never be good enough. *Yes.*

I have everything that I need. *Yes.*

I'm deserving of love. *Yes.*

This just may kill me. *Yes.*

I will survive. *Yes.*

Pay attention to what you affirm to be true, for you will surely manifest the reality in which you believe.

Forgiveness says "yes" to living.

WHISPERS

God speaks in whispers.
Silent brushes of wind
and circumstance that get your attention
and ask you to take notice.

There is so much that I do not understand:
How to sing when I am choking.
How to forget.
How to remember.
How to discern the blessing within the pain.
How to heal so that I may
hold on to greatness and grandeur.

I hate it when all that has wronged me
rises up and snaps
like a leather belt, worn and practiced
injuring others, making me mean.
I really hate that.
It's so sudden; I never see it coming.

Rather,
I wish for softness and stillness,
for the relinquishment of all that no longer matters.
I wish for goodness to linger like the scent of jasmine
on a hot summer day.
It's enough already. It's enough
resenting people and circumstances so far away
that even the scars have dulled with age.

Out there, beyond my small self,
is vastness and forgiveness and fortitude and love.
I long to fall gently into the arms of a loving world.

God speaks in whispers.
Silent brushes of wind and
circumstance that get your attention
and ask you to take notice.

ACCEPTANCE

Accept the path of your life with kindness
and compassion.

The twists and turns, the good and the bad,
are the complicated and intricate
story of your life.

Embrace yourself and your life's story.
That is called "healing."

Life is to be honored and revered.

PRAGMATIC SPIRITUAL PEACE

ACCEPTANCE ALLOWS YOU TO COME TO TERMS with the story of your life. You are what you are. You are not what you are not. And your life is what it is. On some level, those three statements can bring great peace and comfort. But only when you have mourned for what you have lost and felt your genuine anger at the injustice of losing it.

After that comes a pragmatic spiritual peace that fills your soul:

You are what you are.

You are not what you are not.

And life is what it is.

Acceptance is not resignation or settling for less than you deserve. It is coming to terms with reality and redefining events to make meaning out of the past. Your life's path has emerged from the people and events that accepted and embraced you, as well as those people and events that kept you from going where you wanted to go. A life is made up of wonder, excitement, disappointment, beauty, love, loneliness, pain, strength, and dignity. The way you tell the story of your life is a crucial factor in how you perceive your life. Tell the story as if it were an adventure toward learning and wholeness. You are living a good story, and everything negative and every curse contained within it can lead to blessing.

THE TRUTH

The only regrets I have in my life
are the times when I was ungracious.
When my limitations diminished my capacity for love.
When I was so small and filled with self
that my need to be right blinded me to the largeness of the truth.

This is the truth:
Life is short. Often tragic. At times, joyful.
Forgive yourself for all those times when you forgot,
or didn't know, or didn't understand, or ignored,
or didn't have the inner strength to live
this truth.

THE MOON

As a child, I would sometimes be thinking dark thoughts, then, suddenly, I would look up as if I were called by some force and I would be face to face with a beautiful light in the night sky. I took that as a sign that everything would be all right. The bold, constant, lovely light against the dark sky comforted me. It was as if I were having a private conversation with God. I would be deep in thought, riding in the backseat of my parents' car, and suddenly I would look up and see the moon. I would smile, whisper a small prayer, and a sense of hope would be restored to my young spirit. This private moment between the moon, God, and myself has stayed with me. I take the luminous light to heart. It is a guide in the night, a metaphor for hope. Even now, the unexpected sighting of the night light makes me smile.

The phone rang. It was my daughter, Talia. First small talk, and then …

"I feel like one of those dolls."

"What doll?" I asked.

"You know. The kind with the weight on the bottom. You knock it down and it bounces back up." Her voice was soft, steady, and sad.

"At least you bounce back up," I thought.

"I'm tired of being knocked down," she said.

I let my mind wander to all that I wished I could tell Talia, to all that I wanted her to understand: That all the moments you live form the path of your life. That every person and every insult, every exit and every entrance, every blessing and every curse, are the stuff that makes up a life. Accept it. Embrace it. It is *your* story. After coming to terms with it all, bring into balance the different events. Do not let one moment define you. Life is more complex than that. There are markers in your story that are turning points. And having turned, you continue along your way. Tell your story as a tale of triumph and resilience, because you are here to tell it. Take each negative event and tell what good came out of it, what lesson you learned. The way we interpret events can build us up or tear us down. Look at yourself as a beautiful creature with a Divine spark within. Live. Be alive. Release your spark from the darkness that has formed around it. The past brought you to this moment, a moment filled with potential and possibility.

After a moment of silence, I said to Talia, "Don't settle."

"What?"

"Don't settle for a life that is seen as a series of knockdowns."

"But ..."

"Try this," I said, perhaps slightly impatient. "Take a notebook and put a title on each defining moment in your life. Any title. Under that title, list all the bad that came from it. On the next page, list the good that came from it. This is the first step in accepting your life as it is. As it *really* is. Curse and blessing. Being knocked down and ... getting up again."

"That sounds hard to do."

"So is living in sadness."

I looked up from my bed. Although it was early morning, I saw the moon outside my bedroom window. It was full and faint, fading into the brightness of the day.

"It will be fine," I whispered. "It's going to be OK."

Tip Toward Compassion: Concede the Moral High Ground

W<small>E SAT IN AN ELEGANT RESTAURANT</small>, a booth by the water. I ordered the salmon; I think my friend Bill ordered the house special. We often got together to catch up when we were in town for the same convention. As always, he chose the wine. We sipped a lovely Chardonnay as I chatted about a mutual associate that "did me wrong." I was right about her. She was absolutely out to get me, talking behind my back and undermining me, while being sweet as can be to my face. Bill, a lawyer, was a gentle, smart man. He listened, sipped his wine, then said ever so softly, "Concede the moral high ground: You don't have it anyway." I was stunned, then laughed. He smiled and knew he was right. We ordered another glass of wine and we continued to chat as the sun set behind the river's edge, a glorious softness spreading out across the heavens. Brushstrokes of pink and gray illuminated the earth's edge as the fiery red ball slipped out of view, a breath at a time. Just as the last line of fire disappeared into the loveliness of the night, I thought to myself, "But she's wrong and I'm right." And then, I answered myself, "But, maybe, that's not the point."

I looked over the river. The pink and gray had faded into the night just as the sun had done. Nothing remains the same. No day lasts forever. Why hold on to emotions that do not serve us in living a joyful life? As I stared into the fading light, I realized that stars were coming into view. What if, like the constellations, there were a map of the spiritual universe that could guide us, with signposts at forks in the road? What if there were a scale, and on one side of the scale there were truth and justice and on the other side there were truth and compassion? The first time you saw this scale you would be struck by the greatness of its balance: justice steadied by compassion, compassion aided by justice. And on both sides, truth. We are taught to balance the scale with "Justice, justice you shall pursue!" and "The entire world stands on acts of love and kindness." But to live that way can be confusing. To reconcile both truths is maddening, a paradox that baffles the mind. We are taught that right and wrong are black and white—two irreconcilable absolutes. Justice demands one course of action, one emotional response, one moral imperative, while the other side of the scale, the side of compassion, may demand a different course of action or a different emotional or moral response. Abandoning the moral high ground does not mean justifying bad behavior. Do not define yourself by what someone else has done or said, but rather define yourself through your own vision, a vision of wholeness for you and the world. When possible, do not stand in judgment. Tip toward compassion.

I stare at this part of the spiritual map all the time, sometimes letting it tip me toward justice, other times toward compassion. But as I learn more about forgiveness, I tend to tip toward compassion. This is not about who is right and who is wrong or what anyone "deserves." Nor does it deny justice or punishment. We are commanded to pursue a just world. There is nothing easy about compassion in a world that is harsh and that has inflicted wounds upon our hearts. But a world with more compassion would be a lovelier place in which to live. Lovelier. More love.

And that's the point, isn't it? To generate more love, despite it all.

A few years after our conversation that night, Bill died in a car crash on a quiet Minnesota highway. He was on his way to another meeting like the one we had attended. The stark reality of mortality illuminates all that we say and do. If we choose, our life can be as bright as a January moon—full, pregnant, making light in the darkness. And as surely as it rises, so does it set. Do we really need to say that life is short? Life *is* short. And it is unexpected. And we live with the choice to be a light in the darkness, or not. To concede the moral high ground is to say to life and to ourselves: walk softly, with kindness, and you will follow goodness all the days of your life.

Why Is Not the Question

Life is fundamentally unfair and often tragic.

The field looks dry, parched, and yellow, and the tall grass scratches my legs. So do the grasshoppers as they brush up against me, flying past, trying to feed on whatever they can without much delight. Nothing is beautiful here. Everything is vulnerable. A carelessly discarded cigarette could instantly consume what little is left. Even the wasps fly low, heavy from the heat. The only bit of redemption is the early morning dew that clings to the ground. But that, too, is nearly gone.

It's like that sometimes. Dreams seem to disappear like the mist burning in the August morning sun on a field bereft of hope. Life can be hard. Sometimes, in the dark of night, a scream seems to be caught in your throat, choking and suffocating the life out of you. You silently chant over and over again in the core of your being: *Why? It makes no sense. Why?*

At my brother's funeral, I looked around at his friends who were there. It was a surreal experience to be eulogizing my brother. My little brother. I began to do an inventory of all the young people I had known who had died: the seven-year-old boy who drowned in the neighbor's pool, the twenty-something hit by a car while being offered a new job on his cell phone, the forty-something father whose heart stopped beating as he sat on the couch after making breakfast for his family, the recovering addict who flew out of a window in desperation, and the people killed in a house fire or by an overdose or by cancer ... Why do the young die? How do parents bury their children? I don't know.

During the funeral, I could not look into the eyes of my mother, fearing that I would be drawn into them like a free fall down a deep, dark well. The pain from the tragic death of a loved one is so complete, so severe, that it wraps around your soul like plastic wrap, keeping everything in, numbing you to all feeling except profound and all-enveloping sadness and loss.

There is no comforting answer to the question, *why?* And why not? Because there is no God? Because life is cruel and random? Because evil-doers are punished and the good are rewarded in the world to come? Because God "needed" someone and cut his life short? Every answer to *why* leads me to a deeper despondency. Those answers offer no solution, no resolution, no comfort. They make no sense to me. Life's tragedies do not demand an answer to *why*. Rather, they ask *how* and *what*:

How can I make sense of my life?

What have I learned about what is true and important?

How do I turn my pain into compassion for others?

Given what happened to me, how should I change my life?

What am I supposed to do with the profound lesson I have learned?

"Why?" I have no idea. No one really does. This useless question distracts you from what you need to be thinking about. It keeps you in anger. Questions that begin with "how" and "what" lead us toward perseverance and resilience, toward a deeper understanding of life's meaning and purpose.

Tragedy elicits so much pain, and forgiveness can ease some of that pain. We can forgive what was unresolved before a sudden death. We can forgive what was not said or not done. We can forgive our own humanity and sense of helplessness.

STRUGGLING WITH GOD

OUR ANCESTOR JACOB WRESTLED with an angel in the dark of night. A messenger of God. The two struggled, and Jacob was wounded. Their struggle continued until the sun began to rise, and then, just before disappearing, the angel gave Jacob a new name: Israel, one who struggles with God. From that moment forth, Jews have been known as the Children of Israel. So, if you shake your fist at the heavens and scream in the dark of night, "What the hell was that about?" you are in good company: we come from a long line of strugglers. To live, it seems, is to struggle with the Invisible Force. To live is to struggle, and sometimes to be injured, and then to go on.

Speak of forgiveness now. And believe in life. Life whose impulse to survive is so strong that breathing is like a moral imperative. Life that breathes beauty. Life that urges you beyond mere survival. Believe in a life that knows how to call forth light and hope from a dark emptiness, that uses sadness and pain and loss to go forth into the world with a great and abiding compassion. Why? I don't know. What now? Life, despite it all.

Forgiveness is the life force that yearns to break through the darkness.

MOVING ON: THE NEW HOME

I TRIED TO PIECE TOGETHER THE DETAILS of her life by looking through the house to see whether it was suitable for us to buy. It was as if it was stuck in a long-ago decade of avocado, burnt orange, and harvest gold. I saw pictures on the wall—family occasions, men in thick ties, women with pretty dresses and thick glasses, children of various heights, all in black-and-white, with an occasional faded colored portrait. They had been a lovely suburban family. I know that I was just buying her house, but I was also interested in the life that she had, so I began to focus on the details. Self-help books were in every room, and scraps of paper with affirmations and encouraging quotations were taped to mirrors, walls, and the refrigerator. Why did the house feel like a cake mix of nostalgia, sadness, and renewed determination?

"Is she widowed?" I asked the real estate agent. "No," she said. "I hear he left her for his secretary. The house has been on the market for a long time. Priced too high. Wallpaper covering every wall: strawberry designs in the kitchen, Chinese themes in the dining room, glossy geometric patterns in the bathroom. You should have seen the foyer before she painted. Until then, this house just wouldn't 'move.'"

I looked around. What wouldn't "move"? I thought. The house, or the sadness that hung in the air like the smell of must and mothballs? I imagined her shallow breathing. Just how do you place a "fair price" on a lifetime of family and children, on the eventual betrayal that forced this woman to leave what she had worked so hard to create?

The truth is that I loved the house from the moment I entered it. It somehow felt right, like a home. All I needed to do was swing open the windows, let the light in, dust the surfaces and the dark corners, and paint. And all the owner needed to do was believe in her future more than she yearned for her past. So I made an offer. And I would drive by at night. The house would be dark except for the flickering blue TV light in the upstairs bedroom. Looking up, I imagined her in bed, staring at some meaningless show without really watching. I would offer a prayer, not that she would accept my offer, but rather that she would accept the challenge of a new life and the hope that courage would overtake her fear because it was more compelling than her sadness.

She found the courage because she accepted the offer.

I moved in, painted every room, threw out the dusty fringed curtains and let the sunlight bake away the hurt. Air and hope flooded the rooms. Out of respect and reverence, I left the pencil marks that were in the stairway leading to the basement. They had measured the growth of her children over the years. It seemed only right.

Did she forgive him? I'll never know. Can such a thing be forgiven? This I do know:

Forgiveness is never dusty. It cannot breathe in the musty pain of memories. Go into the living room, the room in which you live, that place inside, where the spirit yearns for freedom. Go there and take down the curtains that block the sunlight. They are old and tired. Thinking of what was can keep you captive. It blocks the light and does not let you see outside yourself.

To live fully takes courage. To move forward requires hope.

And anyway, on the other side of the drawn curtain are the sun and the moon rising and setting and the stars all around like points of light telling of possibility.

On the other side of the drawn curtain—life.

Dance Through the Pain

I WASN'T VERY GOOD. Not particularly slender or graceful. Not coordinated or disciplined. In fact, the only qualification I had to be a ballerina was that I was a little girl and being a ballerina was what every little girl wanted to be. So I took lessons. Year after year, my mother signed me up. And year after year, I danced: ballet, tap, toe, character, jazz. Ballet slippers, lamb's wool stuffed into toe shoes, tutus, shiny black tap shoes with silk ties, pink tights with black leotards and, of course, a black patent leather carrying case with a picture of a lovely ballerina on the side. The studio was walled with mirrors and I would stare at my thick, undefined, little-girl body, trying to find a pose or a shape or a moment to the rhythm of Mrs. Tierney's piano. As it turned out, I secretly hated ballet. It was not a happy time for me. It seemed as if everyone else was better than I was. Until one year, when I was picked for a recital. I couldn't believe it. I was going to be a wave, and we even got costumes—sea-green chiffon with sparkly sequins. I was so excited. For weeks, my mother practiced putting my unruly curly hair into a smooth bun, every hair held in place by bobby pins and hair spray.

Then it happened. Days before my recital, I was playing outside and fell down hard on the concrete sidewalk. Knee first. My knee became swollen with blood, gravel, and embedded dirt. Now what would I do? How would I dance with a large, bulky bandage on my knee? How would my pink tights fit over that? How would I manage the grand finale of the wave dance, going down on my knee, hands high in the air? I was inconsolable.

My mother was young and extraordinarily pretty, with blonde hair that was "done" every week by Peggy at the beauty parlor. She found me huddled in the den, crying and bleeding and in total despair. First, she tended to my wound, washing, spraying disinfectant on my knee, finding the right size bandage, talking to me in soft tones. But I would not stop crying, so her voice got louder and firmer. So did my sobs. And there we were, our voices escalating, stuck in our perspectives and our positions:

"It will be OK," my mother insisted.

"No it won't. It's all ruined. I won't be able to go to the recital."

"Yes, you will. It will be OK."

"No, it won't."

"Yes, it will."

"No."

Then it happened. Truth was cast down from the heavens into the mouth of my mother. Although it would take years for me to understand, I was about to receive revelation. My mother held my shoulders tightly. It was like an embrace of love that would never let me go. Our eyes locked in a gaze and she said, "I will bandage your knee and you will put on your costume and step onto the stage. You will look at all the people in the audience and then you will look at me. You will breathe in confidence and you will dance. Dance like a ballerina. Dance as if nothing in the world mattered but the music and the rhythm and the dancers and the audience. Your green chiffon wave will move with your body. You will point your toes, and you will stretch your arms. When it's time for the grand finale, you will perfectly turn on your toes and go down on your knee and smile a big smile because you will have done the most extraordinary thing. You will have danced through your pain."

I did just as I was told.

I still do.

Forgiveness is an intricate dance through pain and anger and loss. Let hope be your partner. Let joy take the lead.

TENDERNESS

Tenderness can hurt.
Like a bruise that marks the spot of internal bleeding.
When life is tender like a bruise,
we turn inward to protect the wound from further insult.
We bandage, cover up, hide, and shield the soft spot.

Or

tenderness can comfort us.
Like a newborn pressed up against your chest,
skin to skin, heart to heart,
it is the rhythm of the world.
It leaves the mark of eternal life upon your soul.

Or

tenderness can enliven.
Like a desert in bloom after winter rains,
it can
flood the barren terrain.
Water flowing seemingly from nowhere;
a sudden and unexpected rush,
tending to that which is parched,
allowing seed to burst forth in color.

Like the pain of being hurt
and the soft touch of vulnerability,
and the unexpected paradox of a desert flower,
forgiveness is tender.

TUG–OF–WAR

THE DAY I MET YOU, you declared, "I am not very spiritual, you know." From then on, we played a friendly game of tug-of-war. Sometimes gentle. Sometimes fierce. Always high stakes—eternity versus oblivion. As it turned out, eternity won. You were about to enter a long, tough battle. Somewhere deep inside, you sensed that life and death would be sharply redefined, and that God and faith could no longer be a "theory" worthy of debate. God was to become your lifeline: There would be no oblivion for you, you decided.

"Cancer," you said as you were leaving class one day. There was fight in your eyes. You would not go gentle into that good night.

I am sure that you thought more than once, "How do I forgive God for this insanity? Cancer makes no godly sense." I know. You tugged on a rope, hoping that if you pulled hard enough you would find faith at the other end. It *is* unfair. It *is* tragic. It *is* maddening. Sometimes it feels like a tug-of-war. I know because time and again I bear witness to the suffering. We have all seen the Angel of Death where we think she does not belong.

You came to class. Every week for a couple of years. You rarely spoke. You always cried, and as time went on your face became softer. After every class, you kissed me goodbye, thanked me, and told me you were OK. But you weren't. You became weaker and weaker. Then came the High Holidays that we knew would be your last. You wanted to stop fighting, to stop tugging at your faith. It was time to let the spirit in you win. Somehow you found the strength to come to temple. On Yom Kippur afternoon, your family wrapped you in a blanket and wheeled you into the healing service. You relaxed into the wheelchair, closed your eyes, and let the song and prayers wash over you and heal you.

Indeed, there was healing. Not of the body—that fight was lost—but of the soul—that fight was won—for you had found faith and inner peace.

Days before you died, you summoned me. Your room was dark, quiet, peaceful. You kissed me one last time. Sometimes I still feel traces of the love it left behind. You sat up. "You came into my life at the exact right time," you whispered. God knows how you found the energy to speak. Your stomach was distended, bloated. Cancer was nearly everywhere, but not in your mind, not in your heart. You felt that you had fought enough. You were asking to die. You weren't angry or morose. Just ready. I told you that you could die if you wanted, but I knew that your will was too tenacious. It would not abide the kind of unconditional surrender that it takes to will yourself to eternal sleep. No, your passing would be up to the Angel of Death. You would not give in. You had to be taken.

And taken you were.

The day I met you, you declared, "I am not very spiritual, you know." From then on, we played a friendly game of tug-of-war. Sometimes gentle. Sometimes fierce. Always high stakes—eternity versus oblivion. As it turned out, eternity won. Sooner or later, it always does.

Forgiveness is the softness of a soul at peace.

FORGIVENESS

Forgiveness is a process, a path without an end,
a bridge that leads to restoration
of what you have lost.

It is a shift of perspective,
a way of being.

Forgiveness is what you do to your soul when you
  choose to live in light rather than in darkness.

HOLDING ON, LETTING GO

Her hair was long, with a slight wave and a henna sheen. Her dark eyes sparkled with intensity as if everything she was about to say would be irreverent or witty or maybe even wise. That's probably why I enjoyed watching her. What an interesting way to react to life: affectionately disrespectful of holiness, with intelligent laughter, always reaching to touch the heart of the matter.

And then she said, "It's an odd thing. Just as I am in awe of those who forgive, I am unwilling to offer forgiveness, as if I am justified in holding on."

And I added, "Or you feel too exposed, too vulnerable to let go."

"Right," she said. "It seems like there are two kinds of people in the world. Those who can forgive and those who can't. I am always in awe of the ones who can forgive. When you forgive, it is as if the whole world has opened up inside you. And when you can't forgive, well, something is shut away forever."

Forgiveness is one of the hardest things we do.

So is not forgiving.

I KNOW NOTHING

THE GRASS WAS PRICKLY AND SCRATCHY on my back as I watched the early evening sky. I was a child, and this patch of grass on my front lawn was one of my favorite places. I knew that the setting sun would cast colors and shadows, hues and images across the sky, and I waited patiently for the drama to unfold. The trees were lacy green against a blue sky and the waiting was like a gracious pause between breaths, like anticipating something great, maybe a redemptive moment when all would be revealed. I wouldn't have put it this way; I was too young. But I think I was waiting for revelation, for God's mystery scripted against the fading light. I was in search of spiritual principle #1, the one that began it all, that moved and held all others, the guiding principle that could begin to explain this stirring that I would later know as my soul. Spiritual principle #1: the answer to sadness and loneliness, the source of joy, the reason for it all.

Years passed. Every time I would think about that yard and of my waiting for another sunset, I would feel the prickly blades of grass on my back, an annoying, itchy, persistent reminder of my elusive search.

It's like that sometimes.

Then it happened. Revelation came, not as I thought it would when I was a child, against the evening sky as the sun set and the stars began to appear. But rather in the form of fiery smoke across the early morning sky. September 11th dramatized unthinkable evil and courage all at once. I stood before a congregation of nearly one thousand people who had come for Rosh Hashanah worship at Northwestern University, outside of Chicago. The scratchy feeling on my back turned into a soul-threatening rash. It was enough already; we all wanted to know the answers to questions that had barely formulated in the few days since the terrorist attacks.

And so I proclaimed that my search was over, that I had found spiritual principle #1:

I know nothing.

I do not know how human beings could have such evil in their hearts. I do not know how people could fly a plane into a building filled with people. I do not know how a man on one of the floors engulfed in fire stood by his friend in a wheelchair as everything fell down around him, instead of running to save himself. I do not know how passengers on a hijacked plane called their loved ones, said goodbye to them, then rushed the cockpit. I know nothing.

Now I realize that anything really worth knowing is, by definition, unknowable. I do not know why some die too soon, or others never find love, or how others are able to forgive.

This I do know: that it is only in this state of not knowing that I am humble enough to approach the mystery.

To forgive, you must embrace the mystery.

THE CHOICE TO BE SUSTAINED

IMAGINE A DARK, MOIST, COOL CAVE. Imagine a hearth and a fire that warms you. The mesmerizing flames draw you into the power of the fire. A thick and nourishing stew is simmering. Around the fire, people are telling stories—tales of heroism and adventure. Stories of survival against all odds. The sounds are soft, like the darkness. Sometimes, someone takes a drum and, like a steady heartbeat, leads everyone in song or a kind of chant that recalls a melody from long ago. Around this fire are healers with medicines and salves that lessen the pain.

Sustainers. They are the ones who tell the stories that bring meaning and understanding. Whose chatter is interesting. Who nourish your soul. Who are neither silly nor trivial. Who can conjure up a melody and a rhythm that help you connect to your past. They are healers. They bring comfort and hold your spirit and your dreams gently in their hearts. All the others should never be invited into the cave.

Despite everything that has been said, not everyone is worthy of your inner circle. There comes a time when you wake up and take stock of the people that surround you. Suddenly you notice that certain people bore you or seem silly or trivial. There are even people whom you realize you don't like very much. And then there are those who don't seem to like you, who are critical or judgmental of you. Now comes the time, you realize, when you must be more discerning.

Forgive yourself for asking this, but are the people around you life-draining or life-affirming?

There is a time in your life that is not about forgiving the inadequacies of others. Rather, it is about refining your circle; it is about the way you spend your time and the people you spend it with. In my book *God Whispers: Stories of the Soul, Lessons of the Heart* (Jewish Lights), I call those people "sustainers." They are the people who see you, *really* see you for who you are and who love you because of that. They *know* you, perhaps better than you know yourself. When you are at your best, they delight in you. When you lose your way, they hold up for you the vision of your higher self. When you look at them, you see in their eyes a mirror of who you are—and you like what you see. Sustainers. They sustain all that is good in you and allow the divine purpose of your life to flow easily through you and through your relationship with them.

Forgiveness is the choice to be sustained and affirmed. Or to move on.

THE GATES OF REPENTANCE

THE RAIN FELL SOFTLY DURING THE NIGHT, gently tapping the silence away. Its steady insistence beckoned the gates: open … open … open. I felt the earth turn on its axis, somehow yielding to the rain, to the Divine Spirit that poured into my heart. Open … open … open.

The book of life, the gates of repentance, the pull toward things divine, toward transcending the silliness, the frailty, the weakness of my humanity. Open, open. I lay quietly in my bed and listened for the sounds and sighs of the world, of those who died today, of those who suffered, who loved, who came into life. I listened for the cracking of the earth and the fury of the sea that can swallow thousands in one immense wave, for the rain softly falling throughout the night.

This was too much for 3:00 a.m. I rose from my bed. "The day will be too long," warned my husband. "There will be time for sleep later," I answered. I rose, drawn to see whether the gates would open this time, entranced by the early morning rain. I boiled water, poured an extra measure of coffee to make it strong, then sweetened it with cocoa and cinnamon. Strong, sweet, spicy: exactly as it should be. The rain stopped. The house became nighttime silent, with an occasional sigh or moan, the way houses do when they settle. I took out a small wooden tray, bought by my friend Rachel, then reached for the creamer given to me by Arna, filled it with 2-percent milk, and enjoyed my coffee in the mug from Carol. We do not need more things, but we buy them for one another— another bud vase, a trivet, a candle, a wine stopper. Signs of friendship, of love, of not being alone. I sat in my blue chair by the window, sipped my coffee, and looked into the night. It was shimmering from the rain, from the suffering in the world, from anticipating the new dawn.

Suddenly, it was safe to think with my soul.

When we are sharp or arrogant or impatient or neglectful, aren't we really scared and lonely and vulnerable? Forgiveness will not come without repentance. They say that the gates of prayer are sometimes closed, but that the gates of repentance are always open. It wasn't prayer that woke me from my sleep. "I am so sorry," I heard my heart cry. Sorry to my husband and my children, to my mother and my father, to my brother, to my friends, to the stranger in my midst. To the one, to the many that cross my path in need. I am so sorry. I have failed to love enough, to be enough, to do enough.

Open. Open. Open.

Forgiveness will not come without repentance.

"*Esa Enai*—I Lift My Eyes"

I am searching for words
For the words that describe,
Make sense, or at least comfort.
Words that summon me from the depths
Of my solitude.

In the night, there is darkness.
Restless attempts to sleep,
Twisting, turning into the shadows.
As I seek a comfortable pose
I bring my knees to my chest
Folding my dreams in half;
Will the crease ever come out?

And in the day there are
Silent attempts to find hope.
Twisting, turning toward the light
As I look for direction, a path, a way.

It is not easy to find the way.

And so
I lift my eyes to the mountains
Heaven lays her head upon the mountaintop
And I begin to climb.

What is the source of my help?
I climb and gaze upon the vistas.
More mountains, more horizons
Never ending moments where Heaven meets earth,
Never-ending possibilities to meet the Divine.

Lift me, carry me, offer me courage.
Help me understand life's sharpest paradox:
That to live is tragic and wonderful,
Painful and awesome, dark and filled with light.

I lift my eyes to the summit
And as I climb I find my help
In the turning and twisting it takes to
Ascend.
I have found a path and it is worn and charted
By all those who are summoned from solitude.
I take their lead.
And I know that in the most essential way
I am being carried up the mountain.
And even now,
Dear God, even now
I am not alone.

LOOKING FOR LIGHT IN THE SHADOWS: *RAKEFET*

I yearn to hide in the shadow of Your wings.
—HASHKEVEINU PRAYER

EVER SINCE I LEARNED THAT I CAN HIDE in the shadow of God's wings, I've been searching. I have searched everywhere for the shadows and the shady spots of the Divine. This was quite a revelation for me—to look for light in the shadows.

A few years ago, my husband, Ezra, and I led a tour to Israel for teenagers from our synagogue. Late one afternoon, we were walking along the rocky paths that led through the mountains in the north. We had no understanding that the flat terrain was actually a plateau of a very high mountain. We just followed what was in front of us. Unknowingly and unsuspectingly, we chatted while following the path. I was walking with the young, beautiful, exceedingly hip and wise woman who was the group's youth director. I'm not sure why, but I decided to tell her about a delicate flower that grows in Israel, the *rakefet*. "It is a small flower," I said. "Usually pink. Its petals are turned sharply backward kind of like the wings of a butterfly. And its shy face looks downward. It's somewhat ironic, I suppose: On one hand, it is rooted, face to the ground. On the other hand, its petals are like wings, ready to take flight."

As Kelly quietly listened, I noticed that Ezra had strayed from the path, and the group of teenagers—scrappy, strong guys—had followed him. He picked up a rock and gently held it in his hand. Knowing my husband, I assumed that he must be explaining volcanic rock and that, in turn, would launch him into the story of the formation of the mountains at the beginning of time. I was instead focused on the timeless beauty of the delicate flower, the *rakefet,* so I stayed on the path.

As Kelly and I continued to walk, my head was down, eyes looking at the ground, like the *rakefet.* "They live in the shadows," I told her. "Solitary, one plant at a time, almost hidden in the crevasses of the rocks, away from direct sunlight. Magnificently sheltered beauty. Israelis name little girls Rakefet, after this flower."

Kelly spoke up. "Why would they name someone after a flower that hides in the shade, looking downward?"

Just then, I looked up. We had approached the mountain's edge. It took my breath away. Suddenly, I became dizzy, disoriented. Now that I had come to the end of solid ground, what supported me was falling away, dramatically disappearing.

It's like that sometimes. You are so sure of where you are, only to find that you are someplace else.

We sat on the cliff, listening to the quiet of the late afternoon. The sun was slipping away and it seemed as if the distractions and noise of the day were giving way to the dusk. A hush was settling in, along with the shadows. Down below the cliff's edge, I saw two hawks flying. I was amazed that I was perched above the flight of the birds, and I realized how fragile it felt to be so high up. Distinctions began to fade and my mind went silent: now, there were merely the hawks, the fading sun, the valley way below us, the path behind us, and me, precariously sitting on the mountain's edge.

Then I saw her. In the crevasses beneath my reach, hiding in the shadows, the *rakefet*. She was gentle, delicate, pink, magenta. Her head was bent down, as if praying on the mountain's edge. But her petals were reaching upward like a butterfly ready to take flight. I pointed out my discovery to Kelly, who smiled, suddenly realizing the magical allure of this flower: a thing of beauty hidden, until it's revealed. Living in the shadows like God, whose mystery is also often not revealed.

Walk to the edge of what you think you know and sit awhile.

Forgiveness is like a flower hiding in the shadows. It is that thing of beauty that has crawled into the cracks of your soul, growing, waiting to be discovered.

IN THE SHADOW OF
YOUR WINGS

Dear God,
I long to find comfort in the shadow of Your wings.
So that I may learn
to risk for the sake of love, for the sake of life.
Teach me, O God, to step softly and gently,
to live with mystery and uncertainty.

O God,
forge a path in my soul that leads toward forgiveness,
and I will follow.

THE CEMETERY

It is cold at the cemetery. I think that the wind must feel the sorrow. Sitting on folding chairs, the family is stunned.

The son said, "It's not like we didn't know that this day would come. Dad was in his eighties, ailing. It's just that I never imagined myself as ... fatherless."

The grave is open. The casket sways as a strong breeze goes by. Tears seem to be stuck in the rim of his eyes.

I whisper to the family, though everyone who is there can hear, "You know, it is traditional at the graveside, moments before the burial, to silently contemplate forgiveness. Ask for forgiveness and you, in turn, accept your father's unspoken request for forgiveness. All people are frail. All relationships are flawed. Love and hurt are so intertwined that sometimes you cannot see the difference. Say you're sorry. Say it's OK."

"How can I say I am sorry to the dead?"

"How can you not?"

"How can I forgive him?"

"How can you not?

"Here. Open up your hand as I place the sandy-colored earth from the Land of Israel in your palm. Feel its texture, its power. What passes through your heart at this moment is both private and universal. The earth in your hand teaches us that grief, love, and loss are shared throughout time and place. Let the earth fall onto the coffin; let it be taken by the wind. See it fly away with the spirit of all that is good in life. See it fall onto the ground, onto the casket. See it return to the earth from where it came. In the end, what passes turns to dust and what is essential is eternal."

Offer a prayer of forgiveness. Your life depends on it.

FROM A MOTHER TO
HER GIRLS

The morning you wake to bury me
you'll wonder what to wear.
The sun may be shining, or maybe it will rain;
it may be winter. Or not.
You'll say to yourself, black, aren't you supposed to
wear black? Then you will remember all the times we went
together to buy clothes: the prom, homecoming,
just another pair of jeans,
another sweater, another pair of shoes. I called you my Barbie dolls.
You will remember how I loved to dress you.
How beautiful you were in my eyes.

The morning you wake to bury me
you will look in the mirror in disbelief.
You'll reach for some makeup. Or not. And you won't believe that
this is the morning you will bury your mother.
But it is. And as you gaze into that mirror, you will
shed a tear. Or not. But look. Look carefully,
for hiding in your expression, you will find mine.
You will see me in your eyes, in the way you laugh.
You will feel me when you think of God,
and of love and struggle.

Look into the mirror and you will see me in a look, or in
the way you hold your mouth or stand, a little bent, or maybe straight.
But you will see me.

So let me tell you, one last time, before you dress,
what to wear. Put on any old thing. Black or red, skirt or pants.
Despite what I told you all these years, it doesn't really matter.
Because as I told you all these years, you are beautiful the way you are.
Dress yourself in honor and dignity.
Dress yourself in confidence and self-love.
Wear a sense of obligation to do for this world,
for you are one of the lucky ones and there is so much to do, to fix.
Take care of each other,
take care of your heart, of your soul.
Talk to God.
Wear humility and compassion.

When you wake to bury me,
put on a strong sense of self, courage, and understanding.
I am sorry. Forgive me. I am sorry.
Stand at my grave clothed in a gown of forgiveness,
dressed like an angel would be, showing compassion
and unconditional love.
For at that very moment, all that will be left of me to give is love.
Love.

LEARNING

All that has happened teaches and enlightens.
Each and every learning
is a choice, a decision on how to proceed.

Let no hurt distract your path from good,
nor pain divert your intention from love.

Learn the divine purpose for your life
and live there.

LETTING GO

IT'S EASY TO RESENT WHAT HAS HAPPENED. We are raised with a sense of fairness, a sense of what is right and what is wrong. Wrong is simply not right: It is not fair that you should experience rejection, cruelty, betrayal. It is not right.

Life, in fact, is fundamentally unfair. What went on in your past, especially during your formative years, truly formed you for good and for bad. I can trace all my character flaws to the people and the circumstances of my youth. I wasn't born edgy, angry, nervous. I am still responding to those things that happened so many years ago, and I continue to resent what was unfair.

But for every negative, a positive can emerge. Learning from resentment does two things. It allows you to acknowledge the injustice of it all. That is an important step away from feeling yourself a victim. It is unfair, and you have the right to resent that. But then ask yourself what blessings are waiting to emerge from those experiences.

That's the power of learning. Dealing with what denies and blocks peace is the foundation of that learning.

This is the stuff of the spiritual path. Reconcile with the truth of your life, with the big, the bad, and the ugly. With beauty and blessing. With the tenacity of your spirit. With weakness. With betrayal. With regret. With the years that have passed. With your destiny. With the love that is trying to get in. If you reconcile with all that, you reconcile with the truth of your life.

The goal is to make peace. To make peace on earth. To make peace among the people in your world. To make peace between you and yours. To make peace with the past. To make peace in the very core of your being.

To make peace with your destiny.

Anything that stands in the way of any of that must be dealt with.

Let it go.

Let it go and it no longer has a hold on you.

Letting it go denies its power over you.

Forgiveness is learning to come to terms with the story of your life and releasing the pain of the past.

WITH ALL MY BEING

IT IS FRIDAY NIGHT AND THE SABBATH HAS BEGUN. As is traditionally done, we have welcomed the angels of Shabbat into our sanctuary and our lives. This symbolic welcoming allows us to shift and settle down and turn toward matters of holiness. At least for a while. I look at the congregation—young and old, joyful and sad, healthy and ill, scared and distracted, humble and humiliated. Everyone is searching for something, brought together by a common longing: to belong, to connect, to be recognized by others and by God. The cantor helps us weave our way through prayer and contemplation, and suddenly we come upon a passage that is less of a prayer and more of a command:

> *You shall love God with all your mind, with all your soul,*
> *and with all your being. Set these words which I command*
> *you today upon your heart ... teach them to your children.*

This is what we are trying to learn: the ultimate path of forgiveness. To love. To love holiness and to connect with the Divine. And having learned it, to teach it diligently to our children. With every aspect of ourselves—mind, body, heart, and soul—we desire to learn, to find a spiritual love, a sense of wholeness and well-being. A sense that we are not alone, that there is a spiritual essence larger than our lives and that is within us and beyond us, now and forever. We yearn to connect to a sense of spirit that allows us to be loving and to live within a loving reality. To learn with all our being is to learn with our mind, body, heart, and soul. Forgiveness can bring us to that level of learning.

Learning involves the mind. Our intellect tries to understand by rationally connecting the dots. We are on a discovery of fact, a creative reordering of empirical truth. The mind is bright with wonder and innovation. It can figure things out. At times, forgiveness can be beyond rational comprehension. Yet, when my mind gets it, I understand. Forgiveness teaches the mind to see the world as a place filled with wonder and mystery and potential, waiting to be discovered and understood.

Learning is of the body. I teach my body to act with care and respect. I move and stretch muscles, ligaments, legs, neck, and arms. I walk and breathe—all with awareness and gratitude for health. Or lacking health, with gratitude for life endured. I tread softly on the earth, kindly, as if it is a gift from God. No waste, no clutter, in partnership with creation. Acting with generosity and compassion is also physical. It is not enough to think about giving. I must physically extend my hand, palm open, filled with what is needed, so I can fill someone else's emptiness with clothes, food, money, work, medicine, safety. Learning is physical. I train my body to act, to dance, to care. Forgiveness teaches the body to tread lightly in this world.

Learning is of the heart. It is an emotional and complicated mixture of past hurt, misperception, and hope, of a longing to love and be loved. We grow into emotional maturity by learning from our emotional immaturity. Through a complicated journey of emotional survival, we learn to feel and to express emotion. We also learn to keep certain emotions to ourselves, when necessary. We learn to name and identify what is "going on" inside of us. We learn what is an overreaction and what is a measured response. We learn when we are responding to the moment or to a past moment. All that is the path to emotional maturity. When we manage to forgive, the balance between a positive and a negative emotional life comes into greater focus. Forgiveness teaches the heart to feel deeply, to let the complicated imperfections of life find their way toward a more compassionate response.

Learning is of the soul. Whether we are asleep or awake, the core of who we are is divine. When forgiveness passes through the mind, body, and heart to the spirit, the world looks remarkably different. There is an internal shift of perspective and we see things through a softer, yet sharper, lens. Mostly, forgiveness is a spiritual state of being, a way of being in the world. Forgiveness teaches and reminds the spirit of a yearning to belong, to connect, to be recognized, to love. And so, having learned all that or, at least, parts of it, we strive for an integrated self, where mind, body, heart, and spirit work together and are aligned in a common cause: the cause of our life.

GOD, DIVINE SOURCE OF LOVE

God, Divine Source of Love,
teach me and I will learn.
Pull me and I will follow.
Open my life to your gifts
so that I may learn of forgiveness and love
with all my mind, with all my soul, and with all my being.

Listen, my child, to the laws of life.

LEARNING FROM IT ALL

Be aware of what you let define you.
You are not the curses or the failures of your life.
Rather, define yourself by blessings and strength.
Do not let the power of what is harsh and negative
be all-powerful.

That which pulls you and pushes you and
denies you and accepts you and
loves you and abandons you
is the story of a life.
Your life.
There is power in blessing and love,
though it is, at times, gentle, quiet, and subtle,
let it be all-powerful.

Pain can be a powerful teacher and
love can be a gentle healer.
We are forever students yearning to learn,
to live a life of enduring good.

God,
like wind against the autumn leaves,
scatter all the pieces of our life.
Show us, dear God,
how to gather and collect
so that the forces in our life may be seen
as seasonal, ever changing, and a lesson in time.

AMBIGUITY AND CONTROL

THE OFFICIAL FLOWER OF THE STATE of Maryland is the black-eyed Susan. Susan's petals are yellow with a slight orange tint. Her eye is, well, black, though one could argue that it is a deep dark brown or maybe even purple. Its power comes from its ambiguity. While driving along Maryland's highways, past lovely green, gentle hills, I sped by the watchful eyes of Susan on the center strip. They were staring at me, one after another. Yellow petals of sunshine with an ambiguous core staring as if they knew me. In fact, they *did* know me, because, like the eye of Susan, the core of my life is also beautiful yet ambiguous, soft yet unyielding: essentially unknowable. This I know. The beauty of my life is like the petal of a flower—clear, bright. And then there is the mystery of my life, which, like the center of this flower, is dark, curious, ambiguous.

It's like that sometimes.

There is a maddening tension between what makes sense and what doesn't. What we yearn to understand at times eludes us. For our entire lifetime, we seem to be on a path toward self-awareness. Why is an essential part of us so elusive? The flow of life appears to be arbitrary: life, death, health, accident, conflict, fortune. There is a perpetual tension between what I know and what I don't know, between what I can understand

and what eludes my understanding. For example, once, a long time ago, my college roommate and I were involved in a crisis that seemed to have no rhyme or reason; no beginning or end; no blessing, only curse. Coming from a Catholic background, she sought out a priest on campus for counseling. "Learn to live with the ambiguity," said Father Bill. That simple thought became one of the guiding beacons of our lives. Throughout the years, Carol and I often retold the story, quoting Father Bill as if his wisdom would ground us, tether us, balance us.

To this day, I appreciate that when something is beyond my power to comprehend and control, I must surrender to some great mystery. Every day, I try to accept the ambiguities in life. Even as I recognize the important and awesome responsibility I have over my actions and reactions, I control the love that comes from my heart, the sincerity that comes from my soul. I control what I choose to focus on. I control my attitude.

Today I surrender and take control because the journey toward forgiveness is mystery and discovery and demands constant navigation.

WHERE IS GOD?

Finally, Rebbe Moshe came to the page
in the Haggadah and began to sing, "Who Knows One?"
Then he asked, "Who can really know the Holy One?
Even the angels ask, 'Where is the dwelling place of the Holy One?'"

Who knows One?
The wise one answers: "I will find You, I will not find You."
And the angels answer:
"The whole world is filled with God's glory."
I can only know God, the Holy One,
Through God's creation and
By the way in which God works through me.
—MARTIN BUBER, *OR HAGANUZ*

SOMETIMES, I FIND YOU.

Wonder and awe emerge from Your hidden place, and I stand tall as I witness beauty and splendor. Sometimes it lasts a while; sometimes it is fleeting. Sometimes it is slight, like a heart flutter. And sometimes it is as dramatic as a canyon carved out between the mountains, exposed by the desert sun. But whichever way it appears, I know that I am in the presence of holiness. And I say, "Amen."

Then, sometimes, I do not find You.

Your absence creates a void, and everything seems insane and upside down. It is as if You are not there—silent, distant, opaque. And I cry and I pray and, like the angels, I turn and ask, "Where is that place where I can find God?" The angels hear my despair and answer, "God is in God's place. The whole world is filled with Divine Glory." And I squint, as if the light were abruptly turned on in a darkened room. And I look again and again, until something makes sense. I search and ask and search some more until, despite all the pain, some bit of holiness emerges.

And having lost, and having found, I am different, changed somehow. Wiser. Deeper. More compassionate, I understand that life is neither black nor white. Not even gray. But rather, that life is like a rainbow high above my head. And like a rainbow, life is dazzling when fully discovered, a dizzying array of truth and falsehood. And I am forced, despite myself and despite all that I have been through, to say, "Amen."

I am not sure why faith is a game of hide-and-seek. But sometimes it is.

LEARNING TO YIELD

Bracha,
a gentle bending,
bowing,
humbling of self-
centeredness.

To ask of God a blessing
is to place Divinity at the core of your being. For this,
bending works best.

Dear God,
I long for Your blessing.
Help me turn aside my pain, fear,
doubt
so that I may be filled with the
light of Your goodness.

My God,
I reach out for Your staff
to guide and comfort me.
Lead me to a stillness of my soul,
so that my life may become
a blessing.

And I know
that there are those who bend because they are
doubled over in pain.
Touch my fingers with kindness, dear One,
that I may wipe their tears with holiness.

Sweet God,
I bow my head in reverence,
yearning to be free of
the silliness that makes me stumble,
the trembling that makes me falter, and
the voices that take me off course.

Bracha,
a gentle bending
bowing
humbling of self-
centeredness.
Oh, that I may be filled with the
light of Your goodness.

RESTORATION

*Time, disappointment, and hurt can
dim the light within.*

*The light of your soul is your gift from God.
It has not gone out.*

*Do whatever it takes to restore your inner light,
even if means letting go
of the darkness.*

REDEMPTION: THE DAY LILIES

WHEN I FIRST MOVED INTO MY HOUSE, the yard looked tired, neglected, overgrown. "She liked it that way," the real estate agent told me. "Since her husband left, she let it grow wild, as if preferring to just let things be, no matter what the consequence."

During the first days in my new home, I would stand at my kitchen sink, happy to do the dishes and just look out the window. Some people dream of a suburban home with a white picket fence. I always wanted a kitchen sink with a large window looking out at a yard, and here I was, at last! June Cleaver!

But the more I looked at my yard, the more I became, well, unsettled. It wasn't what I had in mind. The fence was old, bent and rotten in places. It was the outer border of my new home marking my domestic territory: home to a wife, husband, kids, and a dog. The dirt in the yard was not fertile or holy or particularly attractive. It was hard, cracked, malnourished. The shady part was overgrown with weeds and littered with sticks and fallen branches. And right in the center of this yard, where my kids would want to run or play ball, was a large out-of-control patch of green foliage.

Days passed. I fussed and nested and made the house a home. But the more I looked at the yard, the more it began to feel like a monster of sorts: snarled, angry, and wild, and so I hired a yard guy. "Cut, clear, trim," I instructed, almost indiscriminately. "A manicured yard is the sign of an ordered life," I reasoned. He looked at me, smiled, and proceeded to ignore me. He did a bit here and a bit there and when he was done he proclaimed victory, loaded up his shears, saws, and scissors, and left. Having paid in advance, I was powerless.

Time passed. Autumn arrived. The yard didn't matter, I figured. Let it all die; let the leaves cover the neglected ground. Then came winter and the Chicago cold, snow, and ice, and I began to forget what lay beneath all the white and the slush. And then spring, which always begins with soggy brown ground. And then suddenly the patch in the middle of my yard began to come alive. Day lilies! Healthy green leaves grew from the seemingly dead earth and became wild and tall. This is what rebirth looks like, I thought.

And so it is, year after year. I abandon the day lilies, willy-nilly, leaving them to their own devices. When the summer is dry and hot, they wither quickly. But always in the spring, they reappear. I replant them in a different place in the yard; they not only grow in their new spot but are also reborn in the original bed. I do not water them. They stand tall and green and patiently wait for the rain. They will not die, though I sometimes neglect them. They bloom spring after spring, though I have given them no reason to return.

It's like that sometimes.

A part of my soul lives wild from neglect, sometimes dying, then suddenly living again, always renewing itself like the very act of daily creation. Setting suns, rising moons, setting moons, rising suns—all these are often a blaze of color, dramatic and silent in their ascent and descent. And like the lilies that live in my backyard, my soul runs wild with possibility.

The lilies refuse to die, and so does my spirit. It is strong and resilient, even with constant neglect. Like the day lily, my soul yearns to live. It flowers and dies a mini-death. This is creation, daily renewing itself from within. Each day is filled with possibility and with beauty, despite the past. Each day is another act of creation.

Forgiveness is the profound fact of death and renewal, quiet or dramatic, always a constant cycle, despite it all. Life.

REBIRTH

The world is a clay vessel,
fragile and lovely,
filled with love.
It is easy to break into a thousand pieces
shards of light scattered all around.
Only forgiveness can bring redemption,
a rebirth of new life.

WONDER

Have you ever seen the leaves on a tree quiver as the sun and wind dance to the melody of hope?

I caught a glimpse of this once. It was dusk. The light was ducking beyond the horizon and the branches of the oak trees were swaying in the late afternoon breeze. But I was focusing on making a cup of black tea. It was July and, with my allergies, I could barely catch my breath. I was making tea in the microwave, not particularly thinking or feeling, just watching the cup go in circles while trying to remember how long it took to boil water this way. Then, suddenly, out of the corner of my eye, I saw patches of light flirt with the leaves that were fluttering about like the wings of a green butterfly. Without turning my head or taking my attention away from the teacup, something pulled and tugged at my heart, and I began to wonder.

It's like that sometimes.

To wonder is at once to marvel, to question, to be in awe, to doubt—all at the same time.

How lovely. Such diversity wrapped into one word. To marvel at the goodness and the beauty of life. To deeply question its meaning and purpose, especially at times of horror or boredom or loss. To stand in awe of the miracles and blessings that abound. To doubt all that and more in the shadow of tragedy and sadness with a gasp that simply says, "What the hell was that about?" All that is to wonder.

I was in Oconomowoc, Wisconsin, at a summer camp dedicated to the campers' spiritual and intellectual growth. Sipping my black tea, I asked a group of teenagers what they wondered about. Without raising her hand, one girl asked, "Did you see that awesome sunset yesterday over the lake?" She paused, sipped her soda, and said, "There is so much beauty. Why isn't life always like that?" I wondered what she had experienced to make her blue eyes darken and become distant.

Another girl spoke up. "I was walking around camp and saw all the younger kids and remembered when I first came to camp. I was so scared and excited. It was weird: When did I get so old?"

I looked at her body, slim, tight, yet to yield to love, to birth, to ache, to longing, to pain. We looked at each other and wondered about the passage of time.

The group rambled on about wondering and I began to notice that one boy was sitting very quietly. He was almost never quiet. His grandfather had just been diagnosed with a recurrence of cancer. His brother had died the previous summer of cancer. I glanced at the trees and they were still: no wind, no dance. That kind of wondering sometimes is simply wordless.

To wonder is the foundation of the spiritual life. It is our constant companion. It dances with our spirit, as we wander through the details of our lives, as we question, as we are in awe and marvel, even as we doubt.

Forgiveness lives in the soul that wonders.

PROTECTION

ONCE A FRIEND RETOLD THE STORY of the three little pigs. The vulnerable and frightened pigs sought refuge in the house of straw and the big bad wolf, of course, huffed and puffed and blew the house down. The pigs then built a house of mud and the wolf huffed and puffed and blew the house down. They finally built a house of bricks and were safe from the wolf. No matter how he huffed and puffed, he could not blow the house down. Then my friend said, "You know, the brick house may have kept the wolf out, but it also kept the pigs in."

It's like that sometimes.

We try to protect ourselves from the dangers of the world, only to find ourselves prisoners of our own fear. And, whenever we are unable to forgive, we actually build a fortress that isolates us as well as protects us. It may feel easier to be defensive, but it is not. I have come to believe that it is preferable to risk than to protect. I'd rather chance the hurt than separate myself from the goodness, from the unknown, from the possibilities, from the wild and unpredictable nature of life, from love and relationships. Enormous energy is consumed protecting ourselves from the "maybes" and the "what ifs." That is why fear consumes us. But because everything is possible, there is much energy in love. Fear depletes, diminishes, lessens the magic and the spark in life. Love affirms and multiplies all that is good. Fear is dark. Love is light.

Rather than live within a fortress, I'd prefer walking freely, enjoying the ever-changing landscape. The rocky and mountainous reality of human encounter is, by its very nature, varied, filled with peaks and valleys.

We think that not to forgive is to protect ourselves, like armor surrounding the very vulnerability of the soul. But it is not so. There will always be vulnerability. The soul is created that way. There will always be hurt, and there will always be a chill in the air as the winds shift and the night falls. For there are seasons in nature and in the nature of the human spirit.

To forgive is to see the difference between protection and isolation.

ENERGY

I've come to believe that the struggle to forgive
or not to forgive
is a matter of energy.
Energy wasted.
Energy squandered.
Energy used to hold tight to what is no longer.
Energy that is anger.
Energy that is love.
Energy used to forgive.
Energy redirected or misdirected.
Energy that is like a current,
a stream curving along the rocks, flowing downward,
searching for the lowest place it can penetrate.

ENERGY CAN BE LIGHT, OR MOTION, OR DECAY. And you get to decide how to use your energies.

What fills our minds also fills our souls. Negative thoughts float around, taking up space and focus and energy. It is interesting to imagine what would occupy your mind if the negativity were not present. You see, nature abhors a void. Empty your mind of negativity, and use the space for positive, loving thoughts to take root. And if you can't empty it completely, at least allow a patch of goodness to grow.

And then surely goodness and mercy shall follow you all the days of your life.

FORGIVING GOD

Early one morning, sitting in my living room, I suddenly heard a call and looked up. Across the road sat a cardinal in a tree. He was visible because the trees were still bare from the winter cold. He sat all proud and knowing, with his red chest puffed out. "Red," I thought, "the color of power, of passion, of tenacity." I wondered about the call. It was a silent, outstanding, lovely beckoning. Was he calling me to notice the arrival of spring? "Doesn't he know that it is too early?" I thought. "March can be wicked to the unsuspecting. It may seem like spring, but it's not, not here in Chicago." Yet he was urging me to look up from what I was doing to hear the call. The call spoke of spring and song and hope.

Hope.

That's it. Hope is like the audacity of a cardinal singing of spring a month too soon. Hope is like the call to abandon wintertime melancholy. Hope anticipates a change as fundamental as winter to spring. For a moment, I looked down, deep in thought. Then I looked up, and the cardinal was gone. It was like most revelations—here one moment, gone the next. Elusive. What lingered was the memory. I remembered to hope. And then I had a revelation: I'm not sure that God is to be forgiven as much as simply acknowledged.

As irrational as faith can be, it can also be pragmatic. Irrational because faith does not make sense in the mind, in the brain, in the rational world. Faith requires that your spirit understand this, and this requires a different kind of knowing, a different vocabulary. The same knowing that is needed to understand love, to hear the silent call of a cardinal.

But it is also pragmatic. Faith requires that you look at life without expectation or judgment. It is what it is. The markers on the path of your life appear to have a random quality. A person of faith looks at what seems to be random and discerns a pattern, a picture, a story, a purpose. The painting or poem that is my life has a theme that teaches me of divine truths about my purpose, about the meaning of my life.

Perhaps the problem with forgiveness is that, at times, it does not seem like the rational thing to do. To forgive someone who is undeserving is simply counterintuitive. To forgive God is to assume that we understand the core reason of life, and I know that I do not and that we cannot. We can only acknowledge that life, at its core, is a mystery. We know flashes and slivers and nothing more. So much of life makes little rational sense.

And yet, sure as a bird calling to spring to return, we are also called. Called to live a higher purpose. Called to love. Called to notice beauty and to live in the reality of its grace. We are called out from the darkness and into the heart and soul of life, where meaning is not always understood with the mind but is always understood with the heart and the spirit.

We are called. We need only to look up and listen.

DANCER

Forgiveness is not an emotion
that spontaneously bubbles forth with love and understanding,
erasing all evil and wounds.
That would be impossible, impractical. Even silly.
We tend not to forgive and forget.

Rather,
forgiveness is a spiritual state. A way of being in the world,
a discipline like the
dancer who endures the pain of practice:
toes bleeding, muscles aching, hands reaching upward,
soul flying with grace and joy.

BEAVER CREEK

My FAMILY WENT TO THE MOUNTAINS TO SKI. I went to
write.

For me, the first day was distracting. I tried to settle in with
my thoughts, but my eyes kept staring at the mountains. The
scenery was unfamiliar to me. I was used to writing in a book-
store or in restaurants, or sometimes at my dining room table
with a candle burning as I faced a bare blue wall. But here I
was in the lobby of a hotel nestled at the foot of the Rockies.
The large window exposed the mountain dotted with skiers
and snowboarders. The mountain was powerful, alluring—yet
blinding. "Blinded," I thought. "Blinded from a simple gaze.
Blinded from the light. Blinded from my thoughts." So went
the first day. I would write a word, stare at the mountain,
squint from the blindness, write a sentence, stare, squint.
Blindness. Blankness. Blindness.

It's like that sometimes.

That night was sleepless. I tossed and turned and my heart
was racing; heat was generating as if a fire burned deep within
me. And so it went. My heart raced and it felt like a fire burning in the place where my thoughts should be. I was sweating,
then suddenly cold, panting. Was it the altitude? No more
blindness, just fear. Fear of the creature that inhabited the

night, making my vitals erratic. It was as if a new truth were searing into my soul, and it was terrifying.

The night was unforgiving. Would morning ever come?

Day two. I figured it out. What was bizarre was that skiing was essentially as quiet as falling snow. Unlike other sports, there was no squeaking of shoes on a polished court floor, no audible grunting or shouting out of calls and plays, no crashing sound of helmet, or sticks or balls cracking wood or bodies colliding into piles of flesh and plastic gear, no fans screaming and urging on the players. From the hotel lobby, the window was like a TV screen with the sound off. The lovely swaying, the gentle back and forth, was like watching a dance without music.

Partnership with the mountain, or maybe even with God, looks like a silent ballet flowing side to side, or fast, or slow, or downward.

Then my daughter Shiri crashed into a tree. I didn't see it. I'd been sitting in the hotel lobby drinking hot chocolate, watching the mountain, searching for a metaphor, turning a phrase, seeking thoughts on forgiveness. Shiri was shaken to the core and I, her mother, was oblivious at the moment of her impact. Her ski instructor checked for injury. There was none. Then he got her back on her skis and they skied for another hour and a half. She cried quietly, privately, the entire time. She cried through her descent, and she cried through the rest of the night. She was not hurt. She was angry, indignant, betrayed by the mountain. How could it do this to her? "Chances of that happening are slim to none," the instructor had said. "I just ran out of mountain," said Shiri, her eyes swollen from cold and wind and tears. "I don't think I'll ski tomorrow," she added.

It's like that sometimes.

That night I lay in the darkness. No night sweats, no fires and demons. Just the quiet sound of my daughter in the other room privately crying. It was as silent and as powerful as a skier coming down the mountain. She was angry at the mountain, angry at her tears, angry at losing her struggle with fear. I imagined the mountain that hurt my child: white, unmoving, old as time on earth.

Skiing is a dance between fear and confidence, risk and competence. Fear is respect for the mountain; confidence is respect for yourself. It's OK to fear the mountain, but you should also respect yourself. I prayed for Shiri. Risk is what propels you forward into adventure, and competence is gained because you took the risk. Take the risk, I prayed. Life is a risk. Love is a risk. Live and love over and over again. The next morning, Shiri woke, put on her skis, and went up and down the mountain.

Fear. Confidence. Risk. Competence. Between the earth and our feet is an agreement with God. That is why the ground is called holy.

Day three. I rode the ski lift up Strawberry Hill. As it turns out, I was wrong. Skiing does make a sound. It is a scraping noise. Scrape, whoosh, scrape, whoosh. It is the sound of forging a path in the snow. It is the sound of the dance of give and take, fear and confidence, risk and competence. Back and forth, back and forth. Scraping the path that is uniquely yours, touched by those before you, touched by those after you. Scrape, whoosh. A path in the snow, in the steepness, in the danger, in the glory and beauty of creation. This is the way off the mountain. Scrape, whoosh. The sound of an encounter that is fundamental, effortless, focused. All is one: The mountain and the man. The slope and the child. The journey forward.

Scrape, whoosh: The sound of a soul navigating a path toward a safe base. Scraping the surface to find a safe path. Wind and sun stinging your face, breathing in rhythm with a gentle motion. This is the agreement we make while navigating the complicated path of human relationships. Despite the risk and fear, anything is possible. Even beautiful. Enter the risk and fear and you discover the confidence and competency needed for solid relationships. It is the foundation of intimate, real, probing, complicated human relationships.

Forgiveness is the interaction of fear and confidence, risk and competence.

ZERO VISIBILITY

I WAS TRYING TO GET TO UPSTATE NEW YORK ON A FRIDAY. We probably shouldn't have taken off, but the pilot in a moment of hubris saw a small break in the fierce snowstorm and he went for it. Once in the air, we were stuck. The storm stretched up and down the Eastern seaboard, and there was nowhere to go, not up, not down, not back, not forward. So we circled for an hour, and I kept wondering how much fuel was needed to ride out a storm that was fierce, large, bigger than life itself. With the subtle rocking of the airplane, my mind vacillated between two states: awareness and blankness. I would be acutely aware of everything, every noise, every motion, every expression on the flight attendant's face, every turn of the plane no matter how slight. And then I would be blank, oddly calm and lulled into a trance by the soft hum of the engine and the blinking lights on the plane's wing illuminating the rage of the snow.

I preferred the blank state. Here, there was no fear, no thoughts, just a hum of perpetual motion and blinking red lights attempting to defy whiteout. Time passed. The storm worsened, the circle continued, no one talked, not the pilot, not the flight attendant, not the passengers. We just waited. I looked out my window and saw nothing but white on white.

White snow speeding past a background of white snow. I thought to myself, *so this is what zero visibility looks like.*

Zero visibility looks like death. Or life. It is quiet, white, soft, opaque, beautiful, and terrible.

It's like that sometimes.

We can't seem to see anything at all, only the blankness of our circumstance. We get stuck in a loop, suspended above the world, far from solid ground, blinded by habit, coasting on fumes. But this is the thing: Life is a choice. To live is a choice, or maybe a thousand tiny choices between the status quo and moving on. A choice to laugh or to cry, to live in the present or to live in the past. Eventually, we forgive because the alternative is no longer an option. We forgive because to coast through a storm, without the ability to see beyond the pain of the moment, becomes too precarious, an impossible way to live.

We forgive because when all is said and done, living is like flying in zero visibility. In every moment, there is risk, and perhaps beauty, and perhaps danger. And forgiveness is our best chance to live, really live life.

FEAR AND HOPE

Inside the human heart is fear.
There is also hope.
The two wrestle constantly, like Jacob and his God.
Sometimes one prevails. Sometimes the other.
The struggle is sometimes silent, other times loud.
But it is constant—fear, hope, fear, hope.
Flashes of light and shadow twirling inside us all the time.

It is so much easier when there is love.
When love is in your life
it becomes the context for it all.
Love is the measure of a life well lived,
it is the beacon of possibility.
When you love, the fear is less harsh,
hope a bit stronger.

Love each other.

THE SILENCE BEHIND
THE QUIET

Eᴌɪᴊᴀʜ ᴛʜᴇ ᴘʀᴏᴘʜᴇᴛ; ꜰᴇᴀʀꜰᴜʟ, standing in the mouth of a cave, watching as wind and fire seemed to crack the stone in half. He gazed out into the world, looking for more than what seemed apparent. And suddenly he was told by an inner stirring, by an eternal voice, that God is not in the fire or wind. Rather, God is in a still, small voice. I always loved that thought. I have listened for the stillness during the greatest storms, during the most desperate of times. I have listened.

Once I heard a silence that seemed beyond the quiet.

We began the day with an hour hike down the hills of the Golan Heights that are at the foot of Hermon Mountain in Israel. There were eight families with babies and toddlers, teenagers and grandparents. About thirty in all. On our way down, one place was particularly steep and I walked slowly so as not to lose my footing. I turned to my friend who was waiting patiently behind me and said, "Look at the kids running down this mountain with no fear. This is how we turn children into hikers and hikers into lovers of the land."

We arrived at our destination, the Hermon River. Ezra found a spot with large boulders on the banks and a slow rapid in the river where we could safely play. The fathers were the first to brave the cold water; the children were close behind. The kids were riding the currents, laughing and screaming with joy as their fathers splashed them without mercy and their mothers sat on the boulders at a safe distance, talking to one another. My friend Arna told me to close my eyes and listen to the sounds.

Listening takes practice. Fine-tuning. The first sounds you hear are from the sights you saw before you closed your eyes. But if you sit long enough with your eyes closed, your hearing becomes more sensitive, more acute. I listened first to the laughter and the splashing, then to the river. Beyond the river, I heard birds. And beyond them, the wind. And then, finally and most impressively, I heard the silence behind it all. It was a silence that wrapped itself around all the other sounds like a protective shawl. It was as if this sound, the sound of a pervasive quiet, were the context for all other noises, the container for all other sound. God was so present. The prayer of my heart was overflowing. The power of the Hermon River washed away all that was superfluous and brought me back to that which is essential in life.

Forgiveness offers you stillness. It is the silence behind the quiet.

QUIET MY SOUL,
O HOLY ONE

Still the sounds that torment my mind
and make my heart weep.
Though at times the quiet may be deafening
and the silence lonely, I pray and I wait.
The difference, dear God, is You.
Enter my silences with an inner stirring.
Gently still my fears so that my heart
may hear and my soul may rejoice
and peace can descend like a steady rain at daybreak.
Quiet my soul, O Holy One.
Still the sounds that torment my mind
for love is in the quiet of God's presence
and I long to surrender into the hush.

EPILOGUE

Sometimes the spiritual path is like
an ascending spiral.
Though you may revisit each place along the way,
you are forever pulled higher.
This is called understanding.

Sometimes the spiritual path is like
a descending spiral.
Though you may revisit each place along the way,
you are pulled ever deeper.
This is called wisdom.

Forgiveness is a walk up and down the spiral.
It is a never-ending path.

THE BRIDGE

The entire world is a narrow bridge;
the most important thing is not to fear.
—REBBE NACHMAN OF BRESLOV

IT IS EARLY MORNING AND THE SUN CATCHES DROPS of water on the threads of a spider's web. It really does glisten. The spider is not in sight, just morning dew which will soon disappear. I sit a while; it is as if the beauty was spun to capture me, my attention, my thoughts, my silence. I watch; I observe the rising sun, the burning dew, the web. And then, as if called by an indiscernible urge to move on to the next thing, I leave the web undisturbed. And as I do, I catch a glimpse of the spider, barely visible, hard at work, going in circles, spinning the web that is lovely, strong, and effective. No beginning, no end. A web.

It's like that sometimes.

Forgiveness is like a web. It is not a straight line of cause and effect. Remember—you tend not to forgive and forget. Sometimes you seem to be going in circles, as if you have made little progress. But you have. The progress in the world of the spirit is like a good refrain: it repeats over and over again. You heal, you feel anger, you accept, you learn, you forgive, you heal, and then life continues and you are soon called upon to repeat one or more of these steps. But each repetition is not in vain. It's not that you have not learned a lesson, rather, it's that the lessons of the spirit are learned throughout a lifetime, each time going deeper into the truth of it all.

Forgiveness is like a bridge you seem to cross over and over again. With every crossing, you discover that there is more. More darkness. More to forgive. More to learn. More light than we thought possible, just waiting to be released. More divine revelation to hear, to bear. More pain to feel, to bear. Another memory. Another layer to a memory you already had. All this is part of the journey. But here's the wonderful thing: having crossed the bridge once, it doesn't seem so narrow or dangerous the next time. There is great depth to healing and forgiveness and, one by one, you will discover its various layers.

PERPETUAL CROSSINGS

I walk softly on the damp wooded path.
Mostly I look down
and see the ground beneath my feet is
soft earth, gentle moss,
and, of course, fallen leaves, which,
like angels, have floated to earth
to form a path. A gently lit path in the woods.

And for every chasm along the way,
for every fast-moving stream or deeply cut valley,
a bridge appears.
It seems that there is always
a way across,
a way to get to the other side of fear, of sadness, of disappointment.
There is always a way.

Maybe goodness is the bridge, or beauty is the bridge.
Love is the bridge.
Forgiveness is the bridge.

Of this I am sure:
the path is eternal—it is our life and the length of our days.

And the bridge is eternal—
there are many ways to cross what seems impossible.
Stones in the river, ropes suspended, planks of wood,
arches of steel like love, patience, acceptance,
and forgiveness.

SUGGESTIONS FOR FURTHER READING

Forgiveness, Healing, and Inspiration

Ford, Debbie. *The Right Questions: Ten Essential Questions to Guide You to an Extraordinary Life*. San Francisco: HarperSanFrancisco, 2004.

Ford, Marcia. *Finding Hope: Cultivating God's Gift of a Hopeful Spirit*. Woodstock, Vt.: SkyLight Paths, 2006.

———. *The Sacred Art of Forgiveness: Forgiving Ourselves and Others through God's Grace*. Woodstock, Vt.: SkyLight Paths, 2006.

Kedar, Karyn D. *God Whispers: Stories of the Soul, Lessons of the Heart*. Woodstock, Vt.: Jewish Lights, 2000.

———. *Our Dance with God: Finding Prayer, Perspective and Meaning in the Stories of Our Lives*. Woodstock, Vt.: Jewish Lights, 2004.

Kornfield, Jack. *The Art of Forgiveness, Lovingkindness, and Peace*. New York: Bantam Books, 2002.

Rosner, Elizabeth. *The Speed of Light*. New York: Ballantine Books, 2001.

Shapiro, Rami. *The Sacred Art of Lovingkindness: Preparing to Practice*. Woodstock, Vt.: SkyLight Paths, 2006.

Wiesenthal, Simon. *The Sunflower: On the Possibilities and Limits of Forgiveness*. New York: Schocken Books, 1998.

Wolfson, Ron. *God's To-Do List: 103 Ways to Be an Angel and Do God's Work on Earth*. Woodstock, Vt.: Jewish Lights, 2006.

Wolpe, David. *Making Loss Matter: Creating Meaning in Difficult Times*. New York: Penguin, 1999.

Poetry Collections for Inspiration

Coleman, Barks. *The Soul of Rumi: A New Collection of Ecstatic Poems.* San Francisco: HarperSanFrancisco, 2002.

Housden, Roger. *Risking Everything: 110 Poems of Love and Revelation.* New York: Harmony Books, 2003.

Oliver, Mary. *New and Selected Poems,* Volume 1. Boston: Beacon, 2004.

Perlman, Debbie. *Flames to Heaven: New Psalms for Healing and Praise.* Belgrade: Rad Publishers, 1998.

Rilke, Rainer Maria. *The Selected Poetry of Rainer Maria Rilke.* NP: Vintage, 1989.

Classic Jewish Texts

Buber, Martin. *Or Haganuz (the Hidden Light).* Tel Aviv: Schocken, 1979.

Kaplan, Rabbi Aryeh, trans. *The Lost Princess & Other Kabbalistic Tales of Rebbe Nachman of Breslov.* Woodstock, Vt.: Jewish Lights, 2004.

————. *The Seven Beggars & Other Kabbalistic Tales of Rebbe Nachman of Breslov.* Woodstock, Vt.: Jewish Lights, 2005.

Klagsbrun, Francine. *Voices of Wisdom: Jewish Ideals and Ethics for Everyday Living.* New York: Jonathan David, 2001.

Shapiro, Rami, trans. *Hasidic Tales: Annotated & Explained.* Woodstock, Vt.: SkyLight Paths, 2004.

Weintraub, Simkha. *Healing of Soul, Healing of Body: Spiritual Leaders Unfold the Strength and Solace in Psalms.* Woodstock, Vt.: Jewish Lights, 1994.

Wineman, Aryeh. *Mystic Tales from the Zohar.* Princeton, NJ: Princeton University Press, 1998.

Zaloshinsky, Gavriel, and Shraga Silverstein, eds. *Orchot Tzaddikim: The Ways of the Tzaddikim.* NP: Feldheim, 1995.

Holiday Reading for Inspiration and Healing

Lew, Alan. *This Is Real and You Are Completely Unprepared: The Days of Awe as a Journey of Transformation.* Boston: Little, Brown, 2003.

Peretz Elkins, Rabbi Dov. *Rosh Hashanah Readings: Inspiration, Information and Contemplation.* Woodstock, Vt.: Jewish Lights, 2006.

————. *Yom Kippur Readings: Inspiration, Information and Contemplation.* Woodstock, Vt.: Jewish Lights, 2005.

Wittenberg, Jonathan. *The Eternal Journey: Meditations of the Jewish Year.* New York: Aviv, 2004.

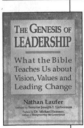

Congregation Resources

The Art of Public Prayer, 2nd Edition: Not for Clergy Only *By Lawrence A. Hoffman*
6 x 9, 272 pp, Quality PB, 978-1-893361-06-5 **$19.99** *(A SkyLight Paths book)*

Becoming a Congregation of Learners: Learning as a Key to Revitalizing
Congregational Life *By Isa Aron, PhD; Foreword by Rabbi Lawrence A. Hoffman*
6 x 9, 304 pp, Quality PB, 978-1-58023-089-6 **$19.95**

Finding a Spiritual Home: How a New Generation of Jews Can Transform the
American Synagogue *By Rabbi Sidney Schwarz*
6 x 9, 352 pp, Quality PB, 978-1-58023-185-5 **$19.95**

Jewish Pastoral Care, 2nd Edition: A Practical Handbook from Traditional &
Contemporary Sources *Edited by Rabbi Dayle A. Friedman*
6 x 9, 528 pp, HC, 978-1-58023-221-0 **$40.00**

Jewish Spiritual Direction: An Innovative Guide from Traditional and Contemporary
Sources *Edited by Rabbi Howard A. Addison and Barbara Eve Breitman*
6 x 9, 368 pp, HC, 978-1-58023-230-2 **$30.00**

The Self-Renewing Congregation: Organizational Strategies for Revitalizing
Congregational Life *By Isa Aron, PhD; Foreword by Dr. Ron Wolfson*
6 x 9, 304 pp, Quality PB, 978-1-58023-166-4 **$19.95**

Spiritual Community: The Power to Restore Hope, Commitment and Joy
By Rabbi David A. Teutsch, PhD 5½ x 8½, 144 pp, HC, 978-1-58023-270-8 **$19.99**

The Spirituality of Welcoming: How to Transform Your Congregation into a
Sacred Community *By Dr. Ron Wolfson* 6 x 9, 224 pp, Quality PB, 978-1-58023-244-9 **$19.99**

Rethinking Synagogues: A New Vocabulary for Congregational Life
By Rabbi Lawrence A. Hoffman 6 x 9, 240 pp, Quality PB, 978-1-58023-248-7 **$19.99**

Children's Books

What You Will See Inside a Synagogue
By Rabbi Lawrence A. Hoffman and Dr. Ron Wolfson; Full-color photos by Bill Aron
A colorful, fun-to-read introduction that explains the ways and whys of Jewish
worship and religious life.
8½ x 10½, 32 pp, Full-color photos, HC, 978-1-59473-012-2 **$17.99** *For ages 6 & up (A SkyLight Paths book)*

The Kids' Fun Book of Jewish Time
By Emily Sper 9 x 7½, 24 pp, Full-color illus., HC, 978-1-58023-311-8 **$16.99**

In God's Hands
By Lawrence Kushner and Gary Schmidt 9 x 12, 32 pp, HC, 978-1-58023-224-1 **$16.99**

Because Nothing Looks Like God
By Lawrence and Karen Kushner
Introduces children to the possibilities of spiritual life.
11 x 8½, 32 pp, Full-color illus., HC, 978-1-58023-092-6 **$16.95** *For ages 4 & up*

Also Available: **Because Nothing Looks Like God Teacher's Guide**
8½ x 11, 22 pp, PB, 978-1-58023-140-4 **$6.95** *For ages 5–8*

> **Board Book Companions to *Because Nothing Looks Like God***
> 5 x 5, 24 pp, Full-color illus., SkyLight Paths Board Books *For ages 0–4*

What Does God Look Like? 978-1-893361-23-2 **$7.99**

How Does God Make Things Happen? 978-1-893361-24-9 **$7.95**

Where Is God? 978-1-893361-17-1 **$7.99**

The Book of Miracles: A Young Person's Guide to Jewish Spiritual Awareness
By Lawrence Kushner. All-new illustrations by the author
6 x 9, 96 pp, 2-color illus., HC, 978-1-879045-78-1 **$16.95** *For ages 9 and up*

In Our Image: God's First Creatures
By Nancy Sohn Swartz 9 x 12, 32 pp, Full-color illus., HC, 978-1-879045-99-6 **$16.95** *For ages 4 & up*

Also Available as a Board Book: **How Did the Animals Help God?**
5 x 5, 24 pp, Board, Full-color illus., 978-1-59473-044-3 **$7.99** *For ages 0–4 (A SkyLight Paths book)*

Children's Books
by Sandy Eisenberg Sasso

Adam & Eve's First Sunset: God's New Day
Engaging new story explores fear and hope, faith and gratitude in ways that will delight kids and adults—inspiring us to bless each of God's days and nights.
9 x 12, 32 pp, Full-color illus., HC, 978-1-58023-177-0 **$17.95** *For ages 4 & up*

Also Available as a Board Book: **Adam and Eve's New Day**
5 x 5, 24 pp, Full-color illus., Board, 978-1-59473-205-8 **$7.99** *For ages 0–4 (A SkyLight Paths book)*

But God Remembered
Stories of Women from Creation to the Promised Land
Four different stories of women—Lillith, Serach, Bityah, and the Daughters of Z—teach us important values through their faith and actions.
9 x 12, 32 pp, Full-color illus., HC, 978-1-879045-43-9 **$16.95** *For ages 8 & up*

Cain & Abel: Finding the Fruits of Peace
Shows children that we have the power to deal with anger in positive ways. Provides questions for kids and adults to explore together.
9 x 12, 32 pp, Full-color illus., HC, 978-1-58023-123-7 **$16.95** *For ages 5 & up*

God in Between
If you wanted to find God, where would you look? This magical, mythical tale teaches that God can be found where we are: within all of us and the relationships between us.
9 x 12, 32 pp, Full-color illus., HC, 978-1-879045-86-6 **$16.95** *For ages 4 & up*

God's Paintbrush: Special 10th Anniversary Edition
Wonderfully interactive, invites children of all faiths and backgrounds to encounter God through moments in their own lives. Provides questions adult and child can explore together.
11 x 8½, 32 pp, Full-color illus., HC, 978-1-58023-195-4 **$17.95** *For ages 4 & up*

Also Available: **God's Paintbrush Teacher's Guide**
8½ x 11, 32 pp, PB, 978-1-879045-57-6 **$8.95**

God's Paintbrush Celebration Kit
A Spiritual Activity Kit for Teachers and Students of All Faiths, All Backgrounds
Additional activity sheets available:
8-Student Activity Sheet Pack (40 sheets/5 sessions), 978-1-58023-058-2 **$19.95**
Single-Student Activity Sheet Pack (5 sessions), 978-1-58023-059-9 **$3.95**

In God's Name
Like an ancient myth in its poetic text and vibrant illustrations, this award-winning modern fable about the search for God's name celebrates the diversity and, at the same time, the unity of all people.
9 x 12, 32 pp, Full-color illus., HC, 978-1-879045-26-2 **$16.99** *For ages 4 & up*

Also Available as a Board Book: **What Is God's Name?**
5 x 5, 24 pp, Board, Full-color illus., 978-1-893361-10-2 **$7.99** *For ages 0–4 (A SkyLight Paths book)*

Also Available: **In God's Name video and study guide**
Computer animation, original music, and children's voices. 18 min. **$29.99**

Also Available in Spanish: **El nombre de Dios**
9 x 12, 32 pp, Full-color illus., HC, 978-1-893361-63-8 **$16.95** *(A SkyLight Paths book)*

Noah's Wife: The Story of Naamah
When God tells Noah to bring the animals of the world onto the ark, God also calls on Naamah, Noah's wife, to save each plant on Earth. Based on an ancient text.
9 x 12, 32 pp, Full-color illus., HC, 978-1-58023-134-3 **$16.95** *For ages 4 & up*

Also Available as a Board Book: **Naamah, Noah's Wife**
5 x 5, 24 pp, Board, 978-1-893361-56-0 **$7.95** *For ages 0–4 (A SkyLight Paths book)*

For Heaven's Sake: Finding God in Unexpected Places
9 x 12, 32 pp, Full-color illus., HC, 978-1-58023-054-4 **$16.95** *For ages 4 & up*

God Said Amen: Finding the Answers to Our Prayers
9 x 12, 32 pp, Full-color illus., HC, 978-1-58023-080-3 **$16.95** *For ages 4 & up*

Theology/Philosophy/The Way Into... Series

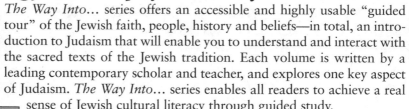

The Way Into... series offers an accessible and highly usable "guided tour" of the Jewish faith, people, history and beliefs—in total, an introduction to Judaism that will enable you to understand and interact with the sacred texts of the Jewish tradition. Each volume is written by a leading contemporary scholar and teacher, and explores one key aspect of Judaism. The Way Into... series enables all readers to achieve a real sense of Jewish cultural literacy through guided study.

The Way Into Encountering God in Judaism
By Neil Gillman
For everyone who wants to understand how Jews have encountered God throughout history and today.
6 x 9, 240 pp, Quality PB, 978-1-58023-199-2 **$18.99**; HC, 978-1-58023-025-4 **$21.95**
Also Available: **The Jewish Approach to God:** A Brief Introduction for Christians
By Neil Gillman
5½ x 8½, 192 pp, Quality PB, 978-1-58023-190-9 **$16.95**

The Way Into Jewish Mystical Tradition
By Lawrence Kushner
Allows readers to interact directly with the sacred mystical text of the Jewish tradition. An accessible introduction to the concepts of Jewish mysticism, their religious and spiritual significance and how they relate to life today.
6 x 9, 224 pp, Quality PB, 978-1-58023-200-5 **$18.99**; HC, 978-1-58023-029-2 **$21.95**

The Way Into Jewish Prayer
By Lawrence A. Hoffman
Opens the door to 3,000 years of Jewish prayer, making available all anyone needs to feel at home in the Jewish way of communicating with God.
6 x 9, 224 pp, Quality PB, 978-1-58023-201-2 **$18.99**

The Way Into Judaism and the Environment
By Jeremy Benstein
Explores the ways in which Judaism contributes to contemporary social-environmental issues, the extent to which Judaism is part of the problem and how it can be part of the solution.
6 x 9, 288 pp, HC, 978-1-58023-268-5 **$24.99**

The Way Into *Tikkun Olam* (Repairing the World)
By Elliot N. Dorff
An accessible introduction to the Jewish concept of the individual's responsibility to care for others and repair the world.
6 x 9, 320 pp, HC, 978-1-58023-269-2 **$24.99**

The Way Into Torah
By Norman J. Cohen
Helps guide in the exploration of the origins and development of Torah, explains why it should be studied and how to do it.
6 x 9, 176 pp, Quality PB, 978-1-58023-198-5 **$16.99**; HC, 978-1-58023-028-5 **$21.95**

The Way Into the Varieties of Jewishness
By Sylvia Barack Fishman, PhD
Explores the religious and historical understanding of what it has meant to be Jewish from ancient times to the present controversy over "Who is a Jew?"
6 x 9, 288 pp, HC, 978-1-58023-030-8 **$24.99**

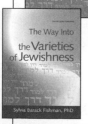

Theology/Philosophy

Christians and Jews in Dialogue: Learning in the Presence of the Other
By Mary C. Boys and Sara S. Lee; Foreword by Dr. Dorothy Bass
6 x 9, 240 pp, HC, 978-1-59473-144-0 **$21.99** *(A SkyLight Paths book)*

The Death of Death: Resurrection and Immortality in Jewish Thought
By Neil Gillman 6 x 9, 336 pp, Quality PB, 978-1-58023-081-0 **$18.95**

Ethics of the Sages: *Pirke Avot*—Annotated & Explained
Translation & Annotation by Rabbi Rami Shapiro
5½ x 8½, 208 pp, Quality PB, 978-1-59473-207-2 **$16.99** *(A SkyLight Paths book)*

Evolving Halakhah: A Progressive Approach to Traditional Jewish Law
By Rabbi Dr. Moshe Zemer 6 x 9, 480 pp, Quality PB, 978-1-58023-127-5 **$29.95**;
HC, 978-1-58023-002-5 **$40.00**

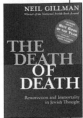

Hasidic Tales: Annotated & Explained
By Rabbi Rami Shapiro; Foreword by Andrew Harvey
5½ x 8½, 240 pp, Quality PB, 978-1-893361-86-7 **$16.95** *(A SkyLight Paths Book)*

Healing the Jewish-Christian Rift: Growing Beyond our Wounded History
By Ron Miller and Laura Bernstein; Foreword by Dr. Beatrice Bruteau
6 x 9, 288 pp, Quality PB, 978-1-59473-139-6 **$18.99** *(A SkyLight Paths book)*

A Heart of Many Rooms: Celebrating the Many Voices within Judaism
By David Hartman 6 x 9, 352 pp, Quality PB, 978-1-58023-156-5 **$19.95**

The Hebrew Prophets: Selections Annotated & Explained
Translation & Annotation by Rabbi Rami Shapiro; Foreword by Zalman M. Schachter-Shalomi
5½ x 8½, 224 pp, Quality PB, 978-1-59473-037-5 **$16.99** *(A SkyLight Paths book)*

A Jewish Understanding of the New Testament
By Rabbi Samuel Sandmel; Preface by Rabbi David Sandmel
5½ x 8½, 368 pp, Quality PB, 978-1-59473-048-1 **$19.99** *(A SkyLight Paths book)*

Keeping Faith with the Psalms: Deepen Your Relationship with God Using the Book
of Psalms *By Daniel F. Polish* 6 x 9, 320 pp, Quality PB, 978-1-58023-300-2 **$18.99**;
HC, 978-1-58023-179-4 **$24.95**

A Living Covenant: The Innovative Spirit in Traditional Judaism
By David Hartman 6 x 9, 368 pp, Quality PB, 978-1-58023-011-7 **$20.00**

Love and Terror in the God Encounter
The Theological Legacy of Rabbi Joseph B. Soloveitchik
By David Hartman 6 x 9, 240 pp, Quality PB, 978-1-58023-176-3 **$19.95**;
HC, 978-1-58023-112-1 **$25.00**

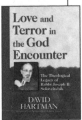

The Personhood of God: Biblical Theology, Human Faith and the Divine Image
By Dr. Yochanan Muffs; Foreword by Dr. David Hartman
6 x 9, 240 pp, HC, 978-1-58023-265-4 **$24.99**

Tormented Master: *The Life and Spiritual Quest of Rabbi Nahman of Bratslav*
By Arthur Green 6 x 9, 416 pp, Quality PB, 978-1-879045-11-8 **$19.99**

Traces of God: Seeing God in Torah, History and Everyday Life
By Neil Gillman 6 x 9, 240 pp, HC, 978-1-58023-249-4 **$21.99**

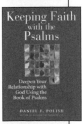

We Jews and Jesus: Exploring Theological Differences for Mutual Understanding
By Rabbi Samuel Sandmel; Preface by Rabbi David Sandmel
6 x 9, 176 pp, Quality PB, 978-1-59473-208-9 **$16.99** *(A SkyLight Paths book)*

Your Word Is Fire: The Hasidic Masters on Contemplative Prayer
Edited and translated by Arthur Green and Barry W. Holtz
6 x 9, 160 pp, Quality PB, 978-1-879045-25-5 **$15.95**

I Am Jewish
Personal Reflections Inspired by the Last Words of Daniel Pearl
Almost 150 Jews—both famous and not—from all walks of life, from all around
the world, write about Identity, Heritage, Covenant / Chosenness and Faith,
Humanity and Ethnicity, and *Tikkun Olam* and Justice.
Edited by Judea and Ruth Pearl
6 x 9, 304 pp, Deluxe PB w/flaps, 978-1-58023-259-3 **$18.99**; HC, 978-1-58023-183-1 **$24.99**
Download a free copy of the *I Am Jewish Teacher's Guide* at our website:
www.jewishlights.com

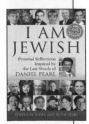

Meditation

The Handbook of Jewish Meditation Practices
A Guide for Enriching the Sabbath and Other Days of Your Life
By Rabbi David A. Cooper Easy-to-learn meditation techniques.
6 x 9, 208 pp, Quality PB, 978-1-58023-102-2 **$16.95**

Discovering Jewish Meditation: Instruction & Guidance for Learning an Ancient
Spiritual Practice By Nan Fink Gefen
6 x 9, 208 pp, Quality PB, 978-1-58023-067-4 **$16.95**

A Heart of Stillness: A Complete Guide to Learning the Art of Meditation
By David A. Cooper 5½ x 8½, 272 pp, Quality PB, 978-1-893361-03-4 **$16.95** (A SkyLight Paths book)

Meditation from the Heart of Judaism: Today's Teachers Share Their
Practices, Techniques, and Faith Edited by Avram Davis
6 x 9, 256 pp, Quality PB, 978-1-58023-049-0 **$16.95**

Silence, Simplicity & Solitude: A Complete Guide to Spiritual Retreat at Home
By David A. Cooper 5½ x 8½, 336 pp, Quality PB, 978-1-893361-04-1 **$16.95**
(A SkyLight Paths book)

The Way of Flame: A Guide to the Forgotten Mystical Tradition of Jewish
Meditation By Avram Davis 4½ x 8, 176 pp, Quality PB, 978-1-58023-060-5 **$15.95**

Ritual/Sacred Practice/Journaling

The Jewish Dream Book: The Key to Opening the Inner Meaning of
Your Dreams By Vanessa L. Ochs with Elizabeth Ochs; Full-color illus. by Kristina Swarner
Instructions for how modern people can perform ancient Jewish dream practices
and dream interpretations drawn from the Jewish wisdom tradition.
8 x 8, 128 pp, Full-color illus., Deluxe PB w/flaps, 978-1-58023-132-9 **$16.95**

The Jewish Journaling Book: How to Use Jewish Tradition to Write
Your Life & Explore Your Soul By Janet Ruth Falon
Details the history of Jewish journaling throughout biblical and modern times, and
teaches specific journaling techniques to help you create and maintain a vital journal,
from a Jewish perspective. 8 x 8, 304 pp, Deluxe PB w/flaps, 978-1-58023-203-6 **$18.99**

The Book of Jewish Sacred Practices: CLAL's Guide to Everyday & Holiday
Rituals & Blessings Edited by Rabbi Irwin Kula and Vanessa L. Ochs, PhD
6 x 9, 368 pp, Quality PB, 978-1-58023-152-7 **$18.95**

Jewish Ritual: A Brief Introduction for Christians
By Rabbi Kerry M. Olitzky and Rabbi Daniel Judson
5½ x 8½, 144 pp, Quality PB, 978-1-58023-210-4 **$14.99**

The Rituals & Practices of a Jewish Life: A Handbook for Personal Spiritual
Renewal Edited by Rabbi Kerry M. Olitzky and Rabbi Daniel Judson
6 x 9, 272 pp, illus., Quality PB, 978-1-58023-169-5 **$18.95**

The Sacred Art of Lovingkindness: Preparing to Practice
By Rabbi Rami Shapiro 5½ x 8½, 176 pp, Quality PB, 978-1-59473-151-8 **$16.99**
(A SkyLight Paths book)

Science Fiction/Mystery & Detective Fiction

Mystery Midrash: An Anthology of Jewish Mystery & Detective Fiction
Edited by Lawrence W. Raphael; Preface by Joel Siegel
6 x 9, 304 pp, Quality PB, 978-1-58023-055-1 **$16.95**

Criminal Kabbalah: An Intriguing Anthology of Jewish Mystery & Detective Fiction
Edited by Lawrence W. Raphael; Foreword by Laurie R. King
6 x 9, 256 pp, Quality PB, 978-1-58023-109-1 **$16.95**

Wandering Stars: An Anthology of Jewish Fantasy & Science Fiction
Edited by Jack Dann; Introduction by Isaac Asimov
6 x 9, 272 pp, Quality PB, 978-1-58023-005-6 **$16.95**

More Wandering Stars: An Anthology of Outstanding Stories of Jewish Fantasy and
Science Fiction Edited by Jack Dann; Introduction by Isaac Asimov
6 x 9, 192 pp, Quality PB, 978-1-58023-063-6 **$16.95**

Spirituality/Lawrence Kushner

Filling Words with Light: Hasidic and Mystical Reflections on Jewish Prayer
By Lawrence Kushner and Nehemia Polen
5½ x 8½, 176 pp, HC, 978-1-58023-216-6 **$21.99**

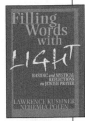

The Book of Letters: A Mystical Hebrew Alphabet
Popular HC Edition, 6 x 9, 80 pp, 2-color text, 978-1-879045-00-2 **$24.95**
Collector's Limited Edition, 9 x 12, 80 pp, gold foil embossed pages, w/limited edition silkscreened print, 978-1-879045-04-0 **$349.00**

The Book of Miracles: A Young Person's Guide to Jewish Spiritual Awareness
6 x 9, 96 pp, 2-color illus., HC, 978-1-879045-78-1 **$16.95** *For ages 9 and up*

The Book of Words: Talking Spiritual Life, Living Spiritual Talk
6 x 9, 160 pp, Quality PB, 978-1-58023-020-9 **$16.95**

Eyes Remade for Wonder: A Lawrence Kushner Reader *Introduction by Thomas Moore*
6 x 9, 240 pp, Quality PB, 978-1-58023-042-1 **$18.95**

God Was in This Place & I, i Did Not Know: Finding Self, Spirituality and Ultimate Meaning 6 x 9, 192 pp, Quality PB, 978-1-879045-33-0 **$16.95**

Honey from the Rock: An Introduction to Jewish Mysticism
6 x 9, 176 pp, Quality PB, 978-1-58023-073-5 **$16.95**

Invisible Lines of Connection: Sacred Stories of the Ordinary
5½ x 8½, 160 pp, Quality PB, 978-1-879045-98-9 **$15.95**

Jewish Spirituality—A Brief Introduction for Christians
5½ x 8½, 112 pp, Quality PB, 978-1-58023-150-3 **$12.95**

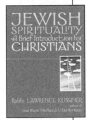

The River of Light: Jewish Mystical Awareness
6 x 9, 192 pp, Quality PB, 978-1-58023-096-4 **$16.95**

The Way Into Jewish Mystical Tradition
6 x 9, 224 pp, Quality PB, 978-1-58023-200-5 **$18.99**; HC, 978-1-58023-029-2 **$21.95**

Spirituality/Prayer

Pray Tell: A Hadassah Guide to Jewish Prayer
By Rabbi Jules Harlow, with contributions from many others
8½ x 11, 400 pp, Quality PB, 978-1-58023-163-3 **$29.95**

Witnesses to the One: The Spiritual History of the *Sh'ma* *By Rabbi Joseph B. Meszler; Foreword by Rabbi Elyse Goldstein* 6 x 9, 176 pp, HC, 978-1-58023-309-5 **$19.99**

My People's Prayer Book Series

Traditional Prayers, Modern Commentaries *Edited by Rabbi Lawrence A. Hoffman*
Provides diverse and exciting commentary to the traditional liturgy, helping modern men and women find new wisdom in Jewish prayer, and bring liturgy into their lives. Each book includes Hebrew text, modern translation, and commentaries from all perspectives of the Jewish world.

Vol. 1—The *Sh'ma* and Its Blessings
7 x 10, 168 pp, HC, 978-1-879045-79-8 **$24.99**

Vol. 2—The *Amidah*
7 x 10, 240 pp, HC, 978-1-879045-80-4 **$24.95**

Vol. 3—*P'sukei D'zimrah* (Morning Psalms)
7 x 10, 240 pp, HC, 978-1-879045-81-1 **$24.95**

Vol. 4—*Seder K'riat Hatorah* (The Torah Service)
7 x 10, 264 pp, HC, 978-1-879045-82-8 **$23.95**

Vol. 5—*Birkhot Hashachar* (Morning Blessings)
7 x 10, 240 pp, HC, 978-1-879045-83-5 **$24.95**

Vol. 6—*Tachanun* and Concluding Prayers
7 x 10, 240 pp, HC, 978-1-879045-84-2 **$24.95**

Vol. 7—Shabbat at Home
7 x 10, 240 pp, HC, 978-1-879045-85-9 **$24.95**

Vol. 8—*Kabbalat Shabbat* (Welcoming Shabbat in the Synagogue)
7 x 10, 240 pp, HC, 978-1-58023-121-3 **$24.99**

Vol. 9—Welcoming the Night: *Minchah* and *Ma'ariv* (Afternoon and Evening Prayer) 7 x 10, 272 pp, HC, 978-1-58023-262-3 **$24.99**

Vol. 10—Shabbat Morning: *Shacharit* and *Musaf* (Morning and Additional Services) 7 x 10, 240 pp, HC, 978-1-58023-240-1 **$24.99**

Current Events/History

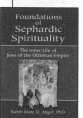

The Story of the Jews: A 4,000-Year Adventure—A Graphic History Book
Written & illustrated by Stan Mack
Witty, illustrated narrative of all the major happenings from biblical times to the twenty-first century. 6 x 9, 288 pp, illus., Quality PB, 978-1-58023-155-8 **$16.95**

Hannah Senesh: Her Life and Diary, the First Complete Edition
By Hannah Senesh; Foreword by Marge Piercy; Preface by Eitan Senesh
6 x 9, 352 pp, HC, 978-1-58023-212-8 **$24.99**

The Jewish Prophet: Visionary Words from Moses and Miriam to Henrietta Szold and A. J. Heschel *By Rabbi Dr. Michael J. Shire*
6½ x 8½, 128 pp, 123 full-color illus., HC, 978-1-58023-168-8
Special gift price $14.95

Foundations of Sephardic Spirituality: The Inner Life of Jews of the Ottoman Empire
By Rabbi Marc D. Angel, PhD 6 x 9, 224 pp, HC, 978-1-58023-243-2 **$24.99**

Judaism and Justice: The Jewish Passion to Repair the World
By Rabbi Sidney Schwarz
6 x 9, 250 pp, HC, 978-1-58023-312-5 **$24.99**

Ecology

Ecology & the Jewish Spirit: Where Nature & the Sacred Meet
Edited by Ellen Bernstein 6 x 9, 288 pp, Quality PB, 978-1-58023-082-7 **$16.95**

Torah of the Earth: Exploring 4,000 Years of Ecology in Jewish Thought
Vol. 1: Biblical Israel: One Land, One People; Rabbinic Judaism: One People, Many Lands
Vol. 2: Zionism: One Land, Two Peoples; Eco-Judaism: One Earth, Many Peoples
Edited by Arthur Waskow
Vol. 1: 6 x 9, 272 pp, Quality PB, 978-1-58023-086-5 **$19.95**
Vol. 2: 6 x 9, 336 pp, Quality PB, 978-1-58023-087-2 **$19.95**

The Way Into Judaism and the Environment
By Jeremy Benstein 6 x 9, 224 pp, HC, 978-1-58023-268-5 **$24.99**

Grief/Healing

Against the Dying of the Light: A Parent's Story of Love, Loss and Hope
By Leonard Fein
5½ x 8½, 176 pp, Quality PB, 978-1-58023-197-8 **$15.99**

Grief in Our Seasons: A Mourner's Kaddish Companion *By Rabbi Kerry M. Olitzky*
4½ x 6½, 448 pp, Quality PB, 978-1-879045-55-2 **$15.95**

Healing of Soul, Healing of Body: Spiritual Leaders Unfold the Strength & Solace in Psalms *Edited by Rabbi Simkha Y. Weintraub, CSW*
6 x 9, 128 pp, 2-color illus. text, Quality PB, 978-1-879045-31-6 **$14.99**

Jewish Paths toward Healing and Wholeness: A Personal Guide to Dealing with Suffering *By Rabbi Kerry M. Olitzky; Foreword by Debbie Friedman.*
6 x 9, 192 pp, Quality PB, 978-1-58023-068-1 **$15.95**

Mourning & Mitzvah, 2nd Edition: A Guided Journal for Walking the Mourner's Path through Grief to Healing *By Anne Brener, LCSW*
7½ x 9, 304 pp, Quality PB, 978-1-58023-113-8 **$19.99**

The Perfect Stranger's Guide to Funerals and Grieving Practices
A Guide to Etiquette in Other People's Religious Ceremonies *Edited by Stuart M. Matlins*
6 x 9, 240 pp, Quality PB, 978-1-893361-20-1 **$16.95** *(A SkyLight Paths book)*

Tears of Sorrow, Seeds of Hope, 2nd Edition: A Jewish Spiritual Companion for Infertility and Pregnancy Loss *By Rabbi Nina Beth Cardin*
6 x 9, 208 pp, Quality PB, 978-1-58023-233-3 **$18.99**

A Time to Mourn, A Time to Comfort, 2nd Edition: A Guide to Jewish Bereavement *By Dr. Ron Wolfson*
7 x 9, 384 pp, Quality PB, 978-1-58023-253-1 **$19.99**

When a Grandparent Dies: A Kid's Own Remembering Workbook for Dealing with Shiva and the Year Beyond *By Nechama Liss-Levinson, PhD*
8 x 10, 48 pp, 2-color text, HC, 978-1-879045-44-6 **$15.95** *For ages 7–13*

Inspiration

God's To-Do List: 103 Ways to Be an Angel and Do God's Work on Earth
By Dr. Ron Wolfson 6 x 9, 150 pp, Quality PB, 978-1-58023-301-9 **$15.99**

God in All Moments: Mystical & Practical Spiritual Wisdom from Hasidic Masters
Edited and translated by Or N. Rose with Ebn D. Leader
5½ x 8½, 192 pp, Quality PB, 978-1-58023-186-2 **$16.95**

Our Dance with God: Finding Prayer, Perspective and Meaning in the Stories of Our
Lives *By Karyn D. Kedar* 6 x 9, 176 pp, Quality PB, 978-1-58023-202-9 **$16.99**

Also Available: **The Dance of the Dolphin** (HC edition of *Our Dance with God*)
6 x 9, 176 pp, HC, 978-1-58023-154-1 **$19.95**

The Empty Chair: Finding Hope and Joy—Timeless Wisdom from a Hasidic Master,
Rebbe Nachman of Breslov *Adapted by Moshe Mykoff and the Breslov Research Institute*
4 x 6, 128 pp, 2-color text, Deluxe PB w/flaps, 978-1-879045-67-5 **$9.95**

The Gentle Weapon: Prayers for Everyday and Not-So-Everyday Moments—
Timeless Wisdom from the Teachings of the Hasidic Master, Rebbe Nachman of Breslov
Adapted by Moshe Mykoff and S. C. Mizrahi, together with the Breslov Research Institute
4 x 6, 144 pp, 2-color text, Deluxe PB w/flaps, 978-1-58023-022-3 **$9.99**

God Whispers: Stories of the Soul, Lessons of the Heart *By Karyn D. Kedar*
6 x 9, 176 pp, Quality PB, 978-1-58023-088-9 **$15.95**

An Orphan in History: One Man's Triumphant Search for His Jewish Roots
By Paul Cowan; Afterword by Rachel Cowan. 6 x 9, 288 pp, Quality PB, 978-1-58023-135-0 **$16.95**

Restful Reflections: Nighttime Inspiration to Calm the Soul, Based on Jewish Wisdom
By Rabbi Kerry M. Olitzky & Rabbi Lori Forman 4½ x 6½, 448 pp, Quality PB, 978-1-58023-091-9 **$15.95**

Sacred Intentions: Daily Inspiration to Strengthen the Spirit, Based on Jewish Wisdom
By Rabbi Kerry M. Olitzky and Rabbi Lori Forman 4½ x 6½, 448 pp, Quality PB, 978-1-58023-061-2 **$15.95**

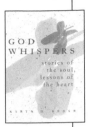

Kabbalah/Mysticism/Enneagram

Awakening to Kabbalah: The Guiding Light of Spiritual Fulfillment
By Rav Michael Laitman, PhD 6 x 9, 192 pp, HC, 978-1-58023-264-7 **$21.99**

Seek My Face: A Jewish Mystical Theology *By Arthur Green*
6 x 9, 304 pp, Quality PB, 978-1-58023-130-5 **$19.95**

Zohar: Annotated & Explained
Translation and annotation by Daniel C. Matt; Foreword by Andrew Harvey
5½ x 8½, 176 pp, Quality PB, 978-1-893361-51-5 **$15.99** *(A SkyLight Paths book)*

Cast in God's Image: Discover Your Personality Type Using the Enneagram and Kabbalah
By Rabbi Howard A. Addison
7 x 9, 176 pp, Quality PB, Layflat binding, 20+ journaling exercises, 978-1-58023-124-4 **$16.95**

Ehyeh: A Kabbalah for Tomorrow
By Arthur Green 6 x 9, 224 pp, Quality PB, 978-1-58023-213-5 **$16.99**

The Enneagram and Kabbalah, 2nd Edition: Reading Your Soul
By Rabbi Howard A. Addison 6 x 9, 192 pp, Quality PB, 978-1-58023-229-6 **$16.99**

Finding Joy: A Practical Spiritual Guide to Happiness *By Dannel I. Schwartz with Mark Hass*
6 x 9, 192 pp, Quality PB, 978-1-58023-009-4 **$14.95**

The Flame of the Heart: Prayers of a Chasidic Mystic *By Reb Noson of Breslov. Translated by*
David Sears with the Breslov Research Institute 5 x 7¼, 160 pp, Quality PB, 978-1-58023-246-3 **$15.99**

The Gift of Kabbalah: Discovering the Secrets of Heaven, Renewing Your Life on Earth
By Tamar Frankiel, PhD 6 x 9, 256 pp, Quality PB, 978-1-58023-141-1 **$16.95;**
. HC, 978-1-58023-108-4 **$21.95**

Kabbalah: A Brief Introduction for Christians
By Tamar Frankiel, PhD 5½ x 8½, 208 pp, Quality PB, 978-1-58023-303-3 **$16.99**

The Lost Princess and Other Kabbalistic Tales of Rebbe Nachman of Breslov
The Seven Beggars and Other Kabbalistic Tales of Rebbe Nachman of Breslov
Translated by Rabbi Aryeh Kaplan; Preface by Rabbi Chaim Kramer
Lost Princess: 6 x 9, 400 pp, Quality PB, 978-1-58023-217-3 **$18.99**
Seven Beggars: 6 x 9, 192 pp, Quality PB, 978-1-58023-250-0 **$16.99**

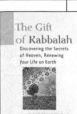

See also *The Way Into Jewish Mystical Tradition* in Spirituality / The Way Into... Series

Holidays/Holy Days

Rosh Hashanah Readings: Inspiration, Information and Contemplation
Yom Kippur Readings: Inspiration, Information and Contemplation
Edited by Rabbi Dov Peretz Elkins with Section Introductions from Arthur Green's These Are the Words
An extraordinary collection of readings, prayers and insights that enable the modern worshiper to enter into the spirit of the High Holy Days in a personal and powerful way, permitting the meaning of the Jewish New Year to enter the heart.
RHR: 6 x 9, 400 pp, HC, 978-1-58023-239-5 **$24.99**
YKR: 6 x 9, 368 pp, HC, 978-1-58023-271-5 **$24.99**

Jewish Holidays: A Brief Introduction for Christians
By Rabbi Kerry M. Olitzky and Rabbi Daniel Judson
5½ x 8½, 144 pp, Quality PB, 978-1-58023-302-6 **$16.99**

Leading the Passover Journey: The Seder's Meaning Revealed, the Haggadah's Story Retold *By Rabbi Nathan Laufer*
Uncovers the hidden meaning of the Seder's rituals and customs.
6 x 9, 224 pp, HC, 978-1-58023-211-1 **$24.99**

Reclaiming Judaism as a Spiritual Practice: Holy Days and Shabbat
By Rabbi Goldie Milgram
7 x 9, 272 pp, Quality PB, 978-1-58023-205-0 **$19.99**

7th Heaven: Celebrating Shabbat with Rebbe Nachman of Breslov
By Moshe Mykoff with the Breslov Research Institute
5⅛ x 8¼, 224 pp, Deluxe PB w/flaps, 978-1-58023-175-6 **$18.95**

The Women's Passover Companion: Women's Reflections on the Festival of Freedom *Edited by Rabbi Sharon Cohen Anisfeld, Tara Mohr, and Catherine Spector*
Groundbreaking. A provocative conversation about women's relationships to Passover as well as the roots and meanings of women's seders.
6 x 9, 352 pp, Quality PB, 978-1-58023-231-9 **$19.99**

The Women's Seder Sourcebook: Rituals & Readings for Use at the Passover Seder *Edited by Rabbi Sharon Cohen Anisfeld, Tara Mohr, and Catherine Spector*
Gathers the voices of more than one hundred women in readings, personal and creative reflections, commentaries, blessings, and ritual suggestions that can be incorporated into your Passover celebration.
6 x 9, 384 pp, Quality PB, 978-1-58023-232-6 **$19.99**

Creating Lively Passover Seders: A Sourcebook of Engaging Tales, Texts & Activities
By David Arnow, PhD 7 x 9, 416 pp, Quality PB, 978-1-58023-184-8 **$24.99**

Hanukkah, 2nd Edition: The Family Guide to Spiritual Celebration
By Dr. Ron Wolfson. Edited by Joel Lurie Grishaver.
7 x 9, 240 pp, illus., Quality PB, 978-1-58023-122-0 **$18.95**

The Jewish Family Fun Book: Holiday Projects, Everyday Activities, and Travel Ideas with Jewish Themes *By Danielle Dardashti and Roni Sarig. Illus. by Avi Katz.*
6 x 9, 288 pp, 70+ b/w illus. & diagrams, Quality PB, 978-1-58023-171-8 **$18.95**

The Jewish Gardening Cookbook: Growing Plants & Cooking for Holidays & Festivals *By Michael Brown* 6 x 9, 224 pp, 30+ b/w illus., Quality PB, 978-1-58023-116-9 **$16.95**

The Jewish Lights Book of Fun Classroom Activities: Simple and Seasonal Projects for Teachers and Students *By Danielle Dardashti and Roni Sarig*
6 x 9, 240 pp, Quality PB, 978-1-58023-206-7 **$19.99**

Passover, 2nd Edition: The Family Guide to Spiritual Celebration
By Dr. Ron Wolfson with Joel Lurie Grishaver 7 x 9, 352 pp, Quality PB, 978-1-58023-174-9 **$19.95**

Shabbat, 2nd Edition: The Family Guide to Preparing for and Celebrating the Sabbath
By Dr. Ron Wolfson 7 x 9, 320 pp, illus., Quality PB, 978-1-58023-164-0 **$19.99**

Sharing Blessings: Children's Stories for Exploring the Spirit of the Jewish Holidays
By Rahel Musleah and Rabbi Michael Klayman
8½ x 11, 64 pp, Full-color illus., HC, 978-1-879045-71-2 **$18.95** *For ages 6 & up*

Life Cycle
Marriage / Parenting / Family / Aging

Jewish Fathers: A Legacy of Love
Photographs by Lloyd Wolf. Essays by Paula Wolfson. Foreword by Rabbi Harold Kushner.
Honors the role of contemporary Jewish fathers in America. Each father tells in his own words what it means to be a parent and Jewish, and what he learned from his own father. Insightful photos.
10¾ x 9⅞, 144 pp with 100+ duotone photos, HC, 978-1-58023-204-3 **$30.00**

The New Jewish Baby Album: Creating and Celebrating the Beginning of a Spiritual Life—A Jewish Lights Companion
By the Editors at Jewish Lights. Foreword by Anita Diamant. Preface by Rabbi Sandy Eisenberg Sasso.
A spiritual keepsake that will be treasured for generations. More than just a memory book, *shows you how—and why it's important*—to create a Jewish home and a Jewish life. 8 x 10, 64 pp, Deluxe Padded HC, Full-color illus., 978-1-58023-138-1 **$19.95**

The Jewish Pregnancy Book: A Resource for the Soul, Body & Mind during Pregnancy, Birth & the First Three Months
By Sandy Falk, MD, and Rabbi Daniel Judson, with Steven A. Rapp
Includes medical information, prayers and rituals for each stage of pregnancy, from a liberal Jewish perspective. 7 x 10, 208 pp, Quality PB, b/w photos, 978-1-58023-178-7 **$16.95**

Celebrating Your New Jewish Daughter: Creating Jewish Ways to Welcome Baby Girls into the Covenant—New and Traditional Ceremonies *By Debra Nussbaum Cohen; Foreword by Rabbi Sandy Eisenberg Sasso* 6 x 9, 272 pp, Quality PB, 978-1-58023-090-2 **$18.95**

The New Jewish Baby Book, 2nd Edition: Names, Ceremonies & Customs—A Guide for Today's Families *By Anita Diamant* 6 x 9, 336 pp, Quality PB, 978-1-58023-251-7 **$19.99**

Parenting As a Spiritual Journey: Deepening Ordinary and Extraordinary Events into Sacred Occasions *By Rabbi Nancy Fuchs-Kreimer* 6 x 9, 224 pp, Quality PB, 978-1-58023-016-2 **$16.95**

Parenting Jewish Teens: A Guide for the Perplexed
By Joanne Doades 6 x 9, 200 pp, Quality PB, 978-1-58023-305-7 **$16.99**

Judaism for Two: A Spiritual Guide for Strengthening and Celebrating Your Loving Relationship *By Rabbi Nancy Fuchs-Kreimer and Rabbi Nancy H. Wiener; Foreword by Rabbi Elliot N. Dorff* Addresses the ways Jewish teachings can enhance and strengthen committed relationships. 6 x 9, 224 pp, Quality PB, 978-1-58023-254-8 **$16.99**

Embracing the Covenant: Converts to Judaism Talk About Why & How
By Rabbi Allan Berkowitz and Patti Moskovitz 6 x 9, 192 pp, Quality PB, 978-1-879045-50-7 **$16.95**

The Guide to Jewish Interfaith Family Life: An InterfaithFamily.com Handbook
Edited by Ronnie Friedland and Edmund Case 6 x 9, 384 pp, Quality PB, 978-1-58023-153-4 **$18.95**

Introducing My Faith and My Community
The Jewish Outreach Institute Guide for the Christian in a Jewish Interfaith Relationship
By Rabbi Kerry M. Olitzky 6 x 9, 176 pp, Quality PB, 978-1-58023-192-3 **$16.99**

Making a Successful Jewish Interfaith Marriage: The Jewish Outreach Institute Guide to Opportunities, Challenges and Resources *By Rabbi Kerry M. Olitzky with Joan Peterson Littman* 6 x 9, 176 pp, Quality PB, 978-1-58023-170-1 **$16.95**

The Creative Jewish Wedding Book: A Hands-On Guide to New & Old Traditions, Ceremonies & Celebrations *By Gabrielle Kaplan-Mayer* 9 x 9, 288 pp, b/w photos, Quality PB, 978-1-58023-194-7 **$19.99**

Divorce Is a Mitzvah: A Practical Guide to Finding Wholeness and Holiness When Your Marriage Dies *By Rabbi Perry Netter; Afterword by Rabbi Laura Geller.* 6 x 9, 224 pp, Quality PB, 978-1-58023-172-5 **$16.95**

A Heart of Wisdom: Making the Jewish Journey from Midlife through the Elder Years
Edited by Susan Berrin; Foreword by Harold Kushner 6 x 9, 384 pp, Quality PB, 978-1-58023-051-3 **$18.95**

So That Your Values Live On: Ethical Wills and How to Prepare Them
Edited by Jack Riemer and Nathaniel Stampfer 6 x 9, 272 pp, Quality PB, 978-1-879045-34-7 **$18.99**

Spirituality

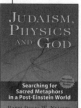

The Adventures of Rabbi Harvey: A Graphic Novel of Jewish Wisdom and Wit in the Wild West *By Steve Sheinkin*
Jewish and American folktales combine in this witty and original graphic novel collection. Creatively retold and set on the western frontier of the 1870s.
6 x 9, 144 pp, Full-color illus., Quality PB, 978-1-58023-310-1 **$16.99**
Also Available: **The Adventures of Rabbi Harvey Teacher's Guide**
8½ x 11, 32 pp, PB, 978-1-58023-326-2 **$8.99**

Ethics of the Sages: *Pirke Avot*—Annotated & Explained
Translation and Annotation by Rabbi Rami Shapiro
5½ x 8½, 192 pp, Quality PB, 978-1-59473-207-2 **$16.99** *(A SkyLight Paths book)*

A Book of Life: Embracing Judaism as a Spiritual Practice
By Michael Strassfeld 6 x 9, 528 pp, Quality PB, 978-1-58023-247-0 **$19.99**

Meaning and Mitzvah: Daily Practices for Reclaiming Judaism through Prayer, God, Torah, Hebrew, Mitzvot and Peoplehood *By Rabbi Goldie Milgram*
7 x 9, 336 pp, Quality PB, 978-1-58023-256-2 **$19.99**

The Soul of the Story: Meetings with Remarkable People
By Rabbi David Zeller 6 x 9, 288 pp, HC, 978-1-58023-272-2 **$21.99**

Aleph-Bet Yoga: Embodying the Hebrew Letters for Physical and Spiritual Well-Being
By Steven A. Rapp. Foreword by Tamar Frankiel, PhD and Judy Greenfeld. Preface by Hart Lazer.
7 x 10, 128 pp, b/w photos, Quality PB, Layflat binding, 978-1-58023-162-6 **$16.95**

Entering the Temple of Dreams: Jewish Prayers, Movements, and Meditations for the End of the Day *By Tamar Frankiel, PhD, and Judy Greenfeld*
7 x 10, 192 pp, illus., Quality PB, 978-1-58023-079-7 **$16.95**

Does the Soul Survive? A Jewish Journey to Belief in Afterlife, Past Lives & Living with Purpose *By Rabbi Elie Kaplan Spitz; Foreword by Brian L. Weiss, MD*
6 x 9, 288 pp, Quality PB, 978-1-58023-165-7 **$16.99**

First Steps to a New Jewish Spirit: Reb Zalman's Guide to Recapturing the Intimacy & Ecstasy in Your Relationship with God *By Rabbi Zalman M. Schachter-Shalomi with Donald Gropman* 6 x 9, 144 pp, Quality PB, 978-1-58023-182-4 **$16.95**

God in Our Relationships: Spirituality between People from the Teachings of Martin Buber *By Rabbi Dennis S. Ross* 5½ x 8½, 160 pp, Quality PB, 978-1-58023-147-3 **$16.95**

Judaism, Physics and God: Searching for Sacred Metaphors in a Post-Einstein World
By Rabbi David W. Nelson 6 x 9, 368 pp, Quality PB, inc. reader's discussion guide, 978-1-58023-306-4 **$18.99;**
HC, 352 pp, 978-1-58023-252-4 **$24.99**

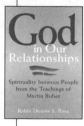

The Jewish Lights Spirituality Handbook: A Guide to Understanding, Exploring & Living a Spiritual Life *Edited by Stuart M. Matlins*
What exactly is "Jewish" about spirituality? How do I make it a part of my life? Fifty of today's foremost spiritual leaders share their ideas and experience with us.
6 x 9, 456 pp, Quality PB, 978-1-58023-093-3 **$19.99**

Bringing the Psalms to Life: How to Understand and Use the Book of Psalms
By Daniel F. Polish 6 x 9, 208 pp, Quality PB, 978-1-58023-157-2 **$16.95;**
HC, 978-1-58023-077-3 **$21.95**

God & the Big Bang: Discovering Harmony between Science & Spirituality
By Daniel C. Matt 6 x 9, 216 pp, Quality PB, 978-1-879045-89-7 **$16.99**

Minding the Temple of the Soul: Balancing Body, Mind, and Spirit through Traditional Jewish Prayer, Movement, and Meditation *By Tamar Frankiel, PhD, and Judy Greenfeld*
7 x 10, 184 pp, illus., Quality PB, 978-1-879045-64-4 **$16.95**
Audiotape of the Blessings and Meditations: 60 min. **$9.95**
Videotape of the Movements and Meditations: 46 min. **$20.00**

One God Clapping: The Spiritual Path of a Zen Rabbi *By Alan Lew with Sherril Jaffe*
5½ x 8½, 336 pp, Quality PB, 978-1-58023-115-2 **$16.95**

There Is No Messiah ... and You're It: The Stunning Transformation of Judaism's Most Provocative Idea *By Rabbi Robert N. Levine, DD*
6 x 9, 192 pp, Quality PB, 978-1-58023-255-5 **$16.99**

These Are the Words: A Vocabulary of Jewish Spiritual Life
By Arthur Green 6 x 9, 304 pp, Quality PB, 978-1-58023-107-7 **$18.95**